More Praise for *Ending Hunger Now*

"Justice to the poor and hungry is a litmus test of our faith. George McGovern, Bob Dole, and Donald Messer make this very clear and, just like Matthew 25, they are straightforward—Jesus asks us, 'Have you fed the hungry or not?' That hunger persists in our world of plenty is a profound moral failure of the human community. I have seen the many faces of hunger, and I have also seen the remarkable ways impoverished people with a little help can become self-sustaining. Their resilience and the continuing commitment of the faith community to live out their beliefs and challenge the social, political, and economic structures that perpetuate hunger and poverty give me hope that hunger will not have the last word. Read this book and take action."
—Rev. John L. McCullough, Executive Director and CEO,
   Church World Service

"If every congregation in America studied *Ending Hunger Now: A Challenge to Persons of Faith,* I believe we would meet that challenge in our time. The book not only is eye-opening, it also opens the heart. In place of the inertia that sets in when we despair of change, the authors inspire hope that an end to hunger is in sight, convincing us to banish old excuses and 'make hunger history.'"
—Bob Edgar, General Secretary, National Council of Churches USA

"The problem of hunger in God's world is not one of capacity, but will. For the person of faith, ameliorating this crisis must be perceived as a command from our Creator. This book provides a passionate proposal and inspirational guide to motivate us to be God's partners in the challenge of *Ending Hunger Now.*"
—Rabbi Jerome M. Epstein, The United Synagogue
   of Conservative Judaism

"Is it possible to end hunger now? George McGovern, Bob Dole, and Donald E. Messer don't ask the question, they just say: We must do it! Is this a challenge? Of course, but for people of faith, everything is possible. Faith accomplishes miracles. By faith the world has been changed. By faith and action we can win the battle; we can make hunger history. We can, and by God's grace we will."
—John Graz, Director, Public Affairs and Religious Liberty,
   Seventh-day Adventist Church

"This important book reminds us that we already have the resources to end hunger in our time. We just need the will. I hope it will be an education, inspiration, and call to action for readers everywhere."
—Marian Wright Edelman, CEO and Founder, Children's Defense Fund

"*Ending Hunger Now* is a power-filled, practical, non-partisan, people-centered, peace-making, perception-bashing production that is not only promising—but possible as well! It is much more than statistics because, as the African saying goes, 'It adds tears to the numbers!'

"I commend the writers and the publisher for putting in our hands and hearts a plan to end hunger by 2030. And the only way to begin this journey of 'ending hunger now' is for you, and especially me, to 'end apathy now!'

"This resource pushes the reader to move on from global guilt trips to practical and doable ways to make the title of this book a reality! And it all starts with me—and you—now!"
—Dr. Rich Bimler, President, Wheat Ridge Ministries,
   www.wheatridge.org

"What a practical and encouraging book, especially for those of us who feel deeply but are not always so confident in our understanding of global issues. Armed with all the experience, wisdom, and inside information most of us lack, the authors make a great case for what I always hoped and suspected to be true: All we lack to end hunger are the moral conviction and the political will to do so, and generating that conviction and will is work we can all do, from wherever we stand, right now."
—Bart Campolo, Founder and Chaplain, Mission Year

"*Ending Hunger Now* will help create vision that will translate into compassion that will move individuals, congregations, businesses, and nations to action . . . and the results could change history, affecting millions of lives for the better!"
—Pastor Brian McLaren, Cedar Ridge Community Church,
   Spencerville, Maryland, and author of *A New Kind of Christian*

Visit www.endinghungernow.org *to discover:*
• detailed author bios
• congregational usage guide
• links to more than 250 hunger organizations
• hunger news and upcoming events
• online discussion forums

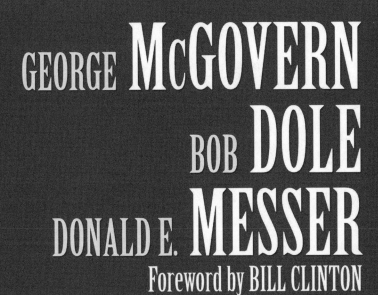

GEORGE McGOVERN
BOB DOLE
DONALD E. MESSER

Foreword by BILL CLINTON

ENDING HUNGER NOW

A Challenge to Persons of Faith

FORTRESS PRESS / MINNEAPOLIS

To

Eleanor, Elizabeth, and Bonnie
three special women
who care deeply about
feeding the hungry of the world

ENDING HUNGER NOW
A Challenge to Persons of Faith

Copyright © 2005 Augsburg Fortress. All rights reserved. Except for brief quotations in critical articles or reviews, no part of this book may be reproduced in any manner without prior written permission from the publisher. Write to: Permissions, Augsburg Fortress, Publishers, P. O. Box 1209, Minneapolis, MN 55440-1209.
    Large-quantity purchases or custom editions of this book are available at a discount from the publisher. For more information, contact the sales department at Augsburg Fortress, Publishers, 1-800-328-4648, or write to: Sales Director, Augsburg Fortress, Publishers, P. O. Box 1209, Minneapolis, MN 55440-1209.
    Scripture passages are from the New Revised Standard Version of the Bible, copyright © 1946, 1952, 1971, 1989 by the Division of Christian Education of the National Council of the Churches of Christ in the USA. Used by permission.
    Portions of chapter two are reprinted with permission of Simon & Schuster Adult Publishing Group from *The Third Freedom* by George McGovern. Copyright © 2001 by George McGovern.

McGovern, George S. (George Stanley), 1922-
  Ending hunger now : a challenge to persons of faith / George McGovern, Bob Dole, Donald E. Messer.
    p. cm.
  Includes bibliographical references.
  ISBN 0-8006-3782-8 (pbk. : alk. paper)
  1. Hunger—Religious aspects—Christianity. I. Dole, Robert J., 1923- II. Messer, Donald E. III. Title.
  BR115.H86.M34 2005
  261.8'326—dc22   2005014327

Cover design by Diana Running; cover photo © Image100/Royalty-Free/CORBIS.
Book design by Michelle L. N. Cook

The paper used in this publication meets the minimum requirements of American National Standard for Information Sciences—Permanence of Paper for Printed Library Materials, ANSI Z329.48-1984. ⊛ ™

Manufactured in the U.S.A.

09   08   07   06   05   1   2   3   4   5   6   7   8   9   10

Contents

Foreword

HUNGER AFFLICTS 300 MILLION
children and a total of nearly one billion people throughout the
world, most of whom live in Asia and Africa. In Sub-Saharan Africa,
the prevalence of hunger is actually increasing. Due to gender discrimination and cultural traditions, women and children often suffer the most.

As President, I worked with two leaders who, three decades earlier, were instrumental in creating the United States' school lunch
program. In 2000, Senator George McGovern and Senator Bob
Dole joined me to announce the creation of the McGovern-Dole
International Food for Education and Child Nutrition Program,
which provided $300 million for nutritious meals to schoolchildren
in developing nations. This initiative gave millions of children desperately needed nourishment and led to dramatic increases in school
enrollment in participating countries. Thanks in large measure to
Dole and McGovern, the program continues today, giving many
poor children a chance for a better future.

For more than thirty years, Senators McGovern and Dole have
worked together to support hunger relief, reaching across party lines
in this critical effort to save lives. Both of them have seen the effects
of hunger, and they understand the devastating impact it can have.

Few Americans have done more to fight hunger at home and
abroad than George McGovern and Bob Dole. Senator McGovern's
involvement with hunger issues dates back to 1961, when he served
as the first Director of Food for Peace under President John F.

Kennedy. I was honored to work in his 1972 Presidential Campaign and am grateful that we have remained friends ever since. During my Administration, I was pleased that he agreed to become Ambassador to the United Nations Agencies for Food and Agriculture in Rome, where he served with great distinction.

Senator Dole has repeatedly demonstrated that combating malnourishment and hunger is more important than partisan politics by partnering with members of both parties to create important anti-hunger legislation. His leadership was crucial in establishing the food stamp program, supplemental food assistance to women and children, and domestic and international school lunch programs. Bob and I had a few disagreements over the years, but not on hunger. I am grateful for his commitment and leadership.

This book makes an important argument about hunger that all concerned citizens should heed: hunger is not just a problem for politicians. We all have an ethical and moral obligation to help people who are suffering. *Ending Hunger Now* is an appeal to people of faith to meet this moral challenge with concrete action. Best of all, Senator McGovern, Senator Dole, and co-author Donald Messer offer specific suggestions for what every concerned citizen can do to contribute to the battle against hunger at home and around our world. At a time in their lives when most people have long been retired, McGovern and Dole are still hard at work, appealing to our minds and hearts, and asking us to follow their lead. All Americans should listen to them, learn, and act.

—The Honorable William J. Clinton,
42nd President of the United States

Introduction

Donald E. Messer

"TO A HUNGRY PERSON," NOTED
Mahatma Gandhi, "God can appear only as a piece of bread." Thus
feeding the hungry always has been at the heart of Christian faith
and ethics, as well as every other major religious and ethical system.

While this book makes an appeal to people of all faiths to join
in ending hunger in the world, we wrote it primarily to help motivate laity and clergy in local congregations to become partners in
God's mission and ministry of combating global hunger. It begins
with the assumption that, regardless of theological or political
persuasion, all people of faith agree on the religious priority of
helping those who lack the basic necessities of food to sustain life.
Disagreements inevitably arise regarding approaches or strategies
for fulfilling this spiritual and moral obligation, but the imperative
of combating human hunger is beyond dispute.

A Need for New Attention to an Old Issue

People of faith need to direct new attention to the issues of world
hunger. The escalating increase of hungry people and food insecurity in both the United States and the world demonstrates the
glaring gap between Christian ideals and human reality. Nearly 850
million people—one-sixth of the population of the Two-Thirds
(sometimes called "developing") world—live malnourished lives.

Demanding special attention are the 300 million hungry children in the world. In the impoverished nations of the world one

in ten children dies before her fifth birthday. Malnutrition contributes to the high death rate as children die from preventable diseases such as diarrhea, acute respiratory infections, malaria, and tuberculosis. Bread for the World reports that more than 36 million U.S. citizens—over 13 million children—live in homes without enough to eat. Volunteer food banks and local charities are stretched beyond their resources.

This book, designed for individual reading and congregational study, highlights new trends and opportunities, offering a challenge to people of faith to become actively engaged spiritually and politically in combating world hunger. Based in practical theology, it provides general information about the hunger crisis in the world and advocates hopeful approaches for addressing it. It does not attempt a comprehensive portrait of the causes and consequences of hunger in today's world. Nor does it pretend to introduce or resolve all of the controversies that surround issues related to world agriculture, environment, globalization, and free trade. Its intent is to serve as a stimulus or catalyst for involving people of faith in exploring and debating these issues.

Global AIDS and International Terrorism

Among the new trends affecting world hunger are global HIV/AIDS and international terrorism. In recent years, various diseases and violence of many types have complicated efforts to end hunger in the world. HIV/AIDS, however, has particularly compounded household food insecurity and decreased national food production. Civil conflicts are common causes of food emergencies, with terrorism posing a special threat for the future.

Clearly the global AIDS pandemic has intensified world hunger. Recent reports from the United Nations Development Program note that "Africa is getting poorer and hungrier" due to high rates of HIV infection.[1] Sub-Saharan Africa is facing the worst hunger crisis in two decades: farmers are dying or are too ill to plant their food. One-third of the entire population is chronically malnourished. Without a good diet and a sustainable food supply, attempts to provide them powerful anti-retroviral medicines will be in vain, as people cannot take medicine on empty stomachs. As I noted in my book *Breaking the Conspiracy of Silence: Christian Churches and the Global AIDS Crisis*, "Hunger and disease create a vicious circle. In many places there is no one left to till the soil and grow the crops because disease and death stalk the land."[2]

Second, possibilities for world peace and a hunger-free world are undermined by international wars and civil conflicts. Preventing conflict and reducing violence in all forms are critical strategies to end hunger. Senator Bob Dole has noted, "Widespread hunger is one of the contributing factors that leads to discontent and creates an environment that is conducive to terrorism."[3] June Kim, Executive Secretary of the United Methodist Committee on Relief's world hunger and poverty program, has stressed that addressing basic needs of food and health care around the world would help reduce problems such as terrorism.[4]

Education and Empowerment of Women

George McGovern and Bob Dole are particularly concerned about feeding children through school lunch programs and thereby contributing to the enhancement of their education. The McGovern-Dole International Food for Education and Child Nutrition Program launched by President Bill Clinton in 2000, and later funded by Congress, seeks to address not only short-term hunger but also some of the societal ills that allow it to endure. An estimated 120 million school-age children are not enrolled in school, often due to hunger or malnutrition. The majority of these children are girls.

Women and female children are disproportionately affected by hunger. The education and empowerment of women in the Two-Thirds world represent an underlying theme of the book. As noted in a *New York Times* article about the McGovern-Dole initiative, "If you feed children, they come to school and stay in school, and they learn better."[5]

The Politics of Hunger

In 1996 world leaders at the United Nations World Food Summit set a goal to cut global hunger in half by 2015 and hunger in the United States in half by 2010. Currently this appears to have little likelihood of being achieved. Instead, the number of hungry people in the world is rising at a rate of about 5 million per year. However, if people and governments make a commitment to *ending hunger now,* then this goal can be reached and surpassed. This book's title is not meant to be utopian but reflects the need for decision and commitment that will eventually make hunger history.

David Beckmann, president of Bread for the World, notes: "Far too many children go to bed hungry each night, be they in Malawi or Milwaukee. The problem is not a lack of food. Hunger is a political problem, and people need to demand change from their elected officials."[6]

We agree with this assessment. Senator George McGovern articulates a vision of a world without malnutrition when he writes, "Hunger has plagued the world for thousands of years. But ending it is a greater moral imperative now than ever before, because for the first time humanity has the instruments in hand to defeat this cruel enemy at a very reasonable cost."[7] McGovern estimates that as little as 19 cents a day could provide children in developing countries a hot school lunch.[8]

Fundamental to this book is an appeal to the biblical, theological, and ethical foundations that motivate Christians and other persons of faith to respond to human need. Theologian Craig L. Nessan has noted that Holy Scripture is "very clear about God's own compassion and concern for the hungry of this world." Speaking at a Lutheran conference, he challenged his audience to imagine "that ending hunger in our world is a real possibility" and to believe "there is enough food in the world and that having access to food is a human right."[9]

The concluding chapter is designed to help persons of faith rethink traditional theological practices along with reappropriating biblical imperatives related to social justice and combating world hunger. Individuals and churches are encouraged to develop and implement a practical theological strategy that embraces both personal involvement and political commitment to end world hunger in our time.

Ways of Using This Book

The practical theology of this book is meant to challenge and engage Christians and other people of faith in addressing world hunger in the United States and internationally as both a spiritual and a moral imperative. As you read it individually or in groups for study and reflection, we hope it will reinforce your work as individuals and as part of churches and organizations dedicated to eliminating hunger in your neighborhoods and around the world.

We were tempted to create a longer book, considering the opportunity to include the substantial writings of Senators Dole and McGovern. However, our purpose was to make the book accessible for local church congregations and others to become more deeply involved in studying the subject of combating world hunger. Thus we created a format of five sessions, including questions following each chapter intended to stimulate reflection and conversation.

Other excellent books address world hunger from various viewpoints. Each chapter includes recommended reading to give you sources for other perspectives or more specialized information. Additionally, several hunger-related Web sites have been included so that you can keep abreast of the latest statistics and updated developments about world hunger.

Since many fine governmental and nongovernmental organizations exist to address world hunger, we have provided a representative, though not exhaustive, listing.

A Word about the Authors

Two of us need no introduction. Senator George S. McGovern and Senator Robert J. Dole are household names and have had eminent careers of public service. Decorated veterans of World War II, they epitomize the best of what Tom Brokaw has called America's "greatest generation." Both men are recognized political leaders, having served in the United States Senate and having been nominees of their parties for the presidency of the United States (McGovern in 1972 and Dole in 1996).

Because these two men often have sharply different political perspectives and champion partisan politics, what many do not realize is that they share a deep friendship, love of country, and strong moral commitments. Throughout their Senate careers and beyond, they have worked in a bipartisan fashion to combat world hunger. They have co-authored legislation over the years to secure programs like food stamps, WIC (Women, Infants, and Children—supplemental food assistance), and more recently the McGovern-Dole International Food for Education and Child Nutrition plan.

Through the decades, both senators have repeatedly spoken out on issues of domestic and world hunger. This book represents yet another effort on their part to marshal people of good will to be concerned advocates for the malnourished of the world.

Standing in the shadow of these two political giants, it has been a privilege and honor for me to work with them in creating this book addressing a core ethical issue of our time. I am deeply grateful that Senator McGovern invited me to join him and Senator Dole in writing this book. My contributions reflect my educational training in Christian social ethics at Boston University and my work as a professor of practical theology at the Iliff School of Theology in Denver, Colorado.

Dole, McGovern, and I are all United Methodists, but we trust this book has an ecumenical, if not interfaith, spirit and perspective. We are grateful that Fortress Press, the ecumenical imprint of a Lutheran publishing house, has chosen to publish it. Throughout this book we have attempted to emphasize a variety of religious organizations and denominations successfully at work addressing domestic and global hunger.

As a native of South Dakota, I have known of McGovern's passion for combating world hunger since my high school days. I met

xiv Ending Hunger Now

him in 1961, when he was the first director of Food for Peace under President John F. Kennedy and he visited southern India, where I was studying. In the years that followed we developed a special friendship, particularly during the ten years I served as president of our alma mater, Dakota Wesleyan University in Mitchell, South Dakota. In many ways he has served as my mentor, demonstrating how to combine politics and public service with a theological ethic oriented to the good of all humanity.

Since my mother was a native of Kansas and both of my parents were lifelong Republicans, I likewise was well-acquainted with Senator Dole's perspectives and policies. Like many Americans I have admired his warm wit, winsome personality, and courageous ability to overcome a wartime disability to give invaluable leadership to this nation.

Incidentally, Dole's parents were Democrats, while McGovern's and mine were Republicans. We have joked that each of us had to find some way to rebel!

A Word of Gratitude

Without the generous spirit and gifted contributions of Senators Dole and McGovern this book could never have been completed. Their willingness to speak out consistently in favor of the impoverished hungry of this world contributes to the moral imperative of this book.

Thanks also are due the staff of Fortress Press for their professional assistance and encouragement at every stage of publication. In particular we want to express our gratitude to Scott Tunseth, Bob Todd, Pamela Johnson, and Michelle L. N. Cook.

Special words of gratitude need to be extended to persons who read the manuscript and offered helpful counsel: Bonnie J. Messer, Maggi Mahan, Ryan Beeman, Sharon Littrell, and Grace A. Messer.

Also, I am grateful for the help of Greg Christy at Dakota Wesleyan and Michael J. Marshall, press secretary to Senator Dole.

And the crowds asked him [John the Baptist], "What then should we do?" In reply he said to them, "Whoever has two coats must share with anyone who has none; and whoever has food must do likewise."
—*Luke 3:10-11*

Hunger is actually the worst weapon of mass destruction. It claims millions of victims each year.
—*Luiz Inacio Lula da Silva, President, Brazil*[1]

1. The New Urgency of an Old Challenge

Donald E. Messer

WHEN THE TRAGIC TSUNAMI OF 2004 swept suddenly across the Indian Ocean, destroying more than 225,000 lives and wrecking the livelihoods of countless millions, a second and third wave of kindness and compassion followed, thanks to the financial and humanitarian generosity of the international community. Aware of the incredible human suffering and tremendous need, individuals and nations stepped forth to offer both immediate

1

and long-term assistance and made plans for creating a warning system so that such a catastrophe might never happen again.

In contrast, the "hunger tsunami" sweeps across the earth *every week,* killing more than 210,000 persons and wrecking the lives of countless millions. But this old challenge of malnutrition and starvation, except in times of extreme famine, rarely draws any headlines or media attention. People and governments tend to accept the status quo of global hunger, even though it leaves more than 850 million people struggling with food insecurity and its dire consequences in terms of health, education, productivity, and poverty.[2] In a given week in the United States, an estimated 7 million people are served at emergency feeding sites.[3]

When you click on the Web site of Stop Hunger Now (www. stophungernow.org), the heartbreaking reality of hunger in the world becomes evident. With the mere movement of my finger, these facts flash on my computer screen:

- Every day 30,000 people die of starvation
- That's 1,250 people every hour
- 20 people every minute
- 1 person every 3 seconds
- You can make a difference with just $1[4]

And then with yet another quick digital click, I move on to something else as if that information about the plight of my global sisters and brothers, nieces and nephews, granddaughters and grandsons, meant nothing. How can I do that?

Why do hundreds of millions of people go hungry in a twenty-first-century world that produces enough food for every man, woman, and child? This apathy and complacency are not new. Centuries ago theologians named it "sloth," or *acedia.* This indifference, inactivity, or internal inhibition to respond to responsibility has been deemed one of the seven deadly sins. Economist Adam Smith once noted that a person could hear about a famine wiping out millions of people in China, yet go to bed and snore peacefully through the night. However, if the same person were to know his little finger were to be amputated the next day, he would spend the night tossing and turning.[5]

In an age when both idealists and realists can envisage a world in which hunger is history, there is new urgency to the old challenge of Jesus, who called persons to feed the hungry, clothe the naked, and care for the sick. There is not a lack of food in the world, but a lack of political will and personal compassion. In the aftermath of the tsunami devastation, Pope John Paul II not only expressed empathy for the victims of that calamity but also appealed for "a vast moral mobilization of public opinion" to stop people from starving in a world with abundant food.[6]

A Forgotten Continent of the Hungry

Hunger tends to be invisible to most of us. Unlike the gripping and ghastly scenes flashed into our homes and hearts following the tsunami, few of us know either the stories or the names of the malnourished. The vast majority live in isolated, rural regions of the so-called developing or Two-Thirds world, distant from the mega-centers of media and government. In fact, some 828 million people make up a "continent" of the hungry, a population exceeding all of Latin America or sub-Saharan Africa.

If we lived in this part of the world, we might very well be the one of every five people who is hungry, one of four who lacks safe drinking water, and one of three who lives on less than $1 a day. The probability of our being homeless, jobless, and suffering from disease are quite high. The chance that our child will die before the age of five is one in ten. We would watch helplessly as our children died from preventable diseases such as diarrhea, acute respiratory infections, or malaria. Our beloved offspring who did live likely would suffer impaired vision, listlessness, stunted growth, and greater susceptibility to disease due to chronic malnutrition. The chances for a good education and a life better than our own would be limited.[7]

During her tenure as president of the American Red Cross, Senator Elizabeth Dole of North Carolina visited Somalia. She reports seeing a boy so malnourished that she thought at first he was dead. When she began to feed him camel's milk, she felt his little bones almost piercing his flesh. She says, "The horror of starvation becomes real—when you can touch it."[8] One child dies every five seconds of hunger and malnutrition, but few of us ever "touch" starvation.

We hear the numbers, but they have no names. Statistics are what Africans call "numbers without tears." It is only when we experience a hungry person or embrace a starving child that we see the reality behind the statistics. Nutritionist Alan Berg describes hunger in humanity this way:

> The light of curiosity absent from children's eyes. Twelve-year-olds with the physical stature of eight-year-olds. Youngsters who lack the energy to brush aside flies collecting about the sores on their faces. Agonizingly slow reflexes of adults crossing traffic. Thirty-year-old mothers who look sixty.[9]

For several years after the 1996 World Food Summit, which set a goal of reducing by half the number of malnourished people by 2015, the numbers did decline, particularly in countries with more rapid economic growth, specifically in the agricultural sectors. China has reduced the number of its hungry citizens by 58 million since the World Food Summit set its goal. Brazil's president launched a comprehensive Fome Zero (Zero Hunger) Project, and Sierra Leone set a bold target of eliminating hunger by the year 2007.

In recent years, however, hunger has again been increasing, especially in nations beset with severe food emergencies and growing HIV/AIDS infections. Hunger elimination has been reversed in sub-Saharan Africa and India, as the global AIDS pandemic has flourished. With the breakup of the Soviet Union and Yugoslavia, the number of undernourished has increased dramatically. For example, in the nations of the former Soviet Union, or Commonwealth of Independent States, the number of hungry people increased from 20.6 to 28.8 million, from 7 to 10 percent of the population.

The vast majority of the world's 852 million malnourished people live in rural regions of the Two-Thirds world. It is not coincidental that most of the 860 million illiterate adults (two-thirds of them women) and the 130 million children (the majority girls) who lack schooling also live in the same rural areas. Hunger and poverty are partners of illiteracy and lack of education. A farmer with only four years of elementary education produces 8.7 percent more, on average, than a farmer with no education. Research in Pakistan has demonstrated that even a small increase in nutrition means that 4 percent more boys and 19 percent more girls start school. Other studies have shown that lack of education decreases productivity and increases vulnerability to hunger. Thus, improving education, especially for women, significantly reduces hunger and malnutrition.[10]

Both food and water are indispensable to life, but globally a billion people live without clean water. When the terrible tsunami swept over the Indian Ocean, Americans were alerted to the dilemma of getting noncontaminated water to the survivors. Emergency rescue efforts were mounted. What the headlines missed was the fact that in the areas affected by the tsunami, 200 million people live without access to clean water all the time, and 850 million lack adequate sanitation services. Every year the death toll from lack of clean water in these areas far exceeds what happened in the December disaster.

Disaster relief experts have noted that the United States spends about $40 million every year for water projects in Asia and Africa, but Americans spend about $10 billion on bottled water domestically. Richard Harris, on National Public Radio, reported that we simply ignore the reality that a child dies every fifteen seconds due to these conditions—a situation equivalent to twenty jumbo jets filled with children crashing every day.[11]

Hunger in the United States

Not to be overlooked is the challenge of addressing hunger in the United States. In 2002 the Census Bureau reported 34.6 million Americans living in poverty, of which 7 million suffer from hunger and are regularly deprived of enough calories. Calling for a "hunger-free America," Senator Elizabeth Dole laments, "It is hard to believe here in America, where we're desperately trying to get a handle on obesity, that there are literally millions of children who don't have enough to eat."[12]

Because children are extremely dependent upon others for food and are highly vulnerable, any discussion of the hungry inevitably and appropriately underscores the plight of hungry children. As theologian Dietrich Bonhoeffer long ago noted, "The test of the morality of a society is how it treats its children." But the leaders of Bread for the World, David Beckmann and Arthur Simon, point out that in America "one child in five lives in poverty" and "one child in five lives in a food-insecure household." Among children under the age of five, the ratio is even higher: one in four.[13] This situation of child neglect cries out for a solution, because, as Marian Wright Edelman of the Children's Defense Fund notes, "God did not make two classes of children," and we must ensure "that no child truly is left behind in our great nation."[14]

A Denver newspaper article recently noted that while national indicators show signs of economic recovery, "there are more hungry, needy kids than ever." The reporter pointed out that 31 percent of all Colorado schoolchildren qualified for free or reduced-price lunches in 2003. This represents a 3.5 percent increase since 2000. Because so many parents either have lost their jobs or have low-paying jobs, the percentage of children qualifying continues to climb yearly. Some 65 percent of children in Denver qualify, while the number decreases in richer suburbs. In western and rural areas of the state, 40 percent meet the need standard.[15]

This story is replicated across America. The U.S. Conference of Mayors noted that in a 2004 survey of twenty-seven cities, food requests increased by 14 percent and appeals for shelter by 6 percent over the previous year. Typically Americans think these issues are centered primarily in major metropolitan cities like New York, Detroit, Los Angeles, and Chicago. But the mayors noted the greatest spike in demand was in Louisville, Kentucky (with a 32 percent increase), and Salt Lake City, Utah (with a 31 percent increase).[16] The federal food stamp program cost $24 billion in 2003, but as the federal deficit grows, expanding increases will be difficult.

Food Insecurity and HIV/AIDS

A primary illustration of how there is new urgency to the old challenge of feeding the hungry is how world hunger and the global HIV/AIDS pandemic are inextricably intertwined. Food security is imperative in the prevention, care, and treatment of HIV/AIDS.[17]

An estimated 43 million people currently live with HIV/AIDS. Nine additional people are infected every minute. No cure or vaccine exists, and none appears to be likely in the foreseeable future. More people will die from AIDS during this decade than from all the wars and disasters of the past fifty years. Former U.S. Secretary of State Colin Powell has noted: "No war on the face of the world is more destructive than the AIDS pandemic. I was a soldier, but I know of no enemy in war more insidious or vicious than AIDS, an enemy that poses a clear and present danger to the world."[18]

HIV/AIDS causes food insecurity. In southern Africa many regions are left with only the elderly and the young, since those adults who would normally be the most productive are too ill to work in the fields. By 2020 it is estimated that one-fifth of the agricultural labor force in southern Africa will have been lost to the disease. One study in Zimbabwe demonstrated that maize production fell by 61 percent in households that suffered an AIDS-related death.

AIDS diminishes investment in agriculture. It strips households of assets: families are forced to sell off what little they have to pay for medical and funeral expenses, or simply to survive. It forces children, particularly girls, to withdraw from school to work or care for ill parents. It cuts off the transfer of essential skills and knowledge from one generation to the next. In two districts in Kenya affected by AIDS, a study found that only 7 percent of orphans heading farm households had adequate agricultural knowledge.[19]

HIV/AIDS is not only a cause but also a consequence of hunger. Many are forced to move from rural areas to crowded urban slums, where HIV infection rates are high. Because people are hungry, they often adopt risky behaviors that lead to infection. Impoverished widows and young children may in desperation become involved in survival sex in order to earn money to feed their families. A young Baptist evangelist told me that in northeast India she knew many desperate women who had no alternative to sex work once their husbands died. Lacking literacy and education, they had no resources or employment opportunities so they could feed their children. In Haiti, a twelve-year-old child involved in prostitution was asked whether she knew she could get AIDS. She answered, "I am afraid. But even if I get AIDS, I'll live a few years, won't I? You see, my family has no food for tomorrow."[20]

Food is crucial for effective programs of HIV/AIDS education, prevention, care, and treatment. For example, in Uganda, studies indicate that people who complete primary school are only half as likely to contract HIV as those who drop out, and those who finish a secondary education are 15 percent as likely to become infected as those who fail to finish school.[21]

Malnourished persons cannot take anti-retroviral medicines—empty stomachs cannot tolerate powerful pills. HIV develops more quickly into full-blown AIDS in people suffering from undernourishment, as opportunistic infections take advantage of a weakened body. As medical scientists know, "Once the disease takes hold, nutrient absorption is reduced, appetite and metabolism are disrupted and muscles, organs, and other tissues waste away. People living with HIV/AIDS need to eat considerably more food to fight the illness, counteract weight loss and extend a productive life."[22]

If we are to conquer global HIV/AIDS, than we must eliminate hunger from the face of the earth. Food security may be the first and most important HIV prevention strategy and response to AIDS.

Biblical and Theological Perspectives

Feeding the hungry is a challenge for all persons of faith. It is not simply a Christian mandate; it is reflected in every religious tradition. The Hebrew Bible, the Jewish sacred text, emphasizes that God has created a world rich in abundance and meant for all people. Islam affirms both almsgiving and fasting as pillars of faith, emphasizing the importance of sharing. Buddhists are called to compassion, and Hindus are expected to share with the hungry.

Within the Jewish and Christian traditions, at least eight over-lapping themes can be briefly underscored. At the core of each of theme is the basic understanding that justice and love of neighbor call people of faith to feed the hungry. These overarching values permeate the Hebrew Bible and the New Testament.

First and foremost is the reminder that God has created a world rich in abundance and meant for all people. The creation story in Genesis, which features the abundance of the Garden of Eden, reminds Jews and Christians of God's intention. Truly, "the earth and its fullness are the Lord's" (1 Corinthians 10:26).

Food and eating are central themes of the New Testament. Many of the parables and other key stories of the Bible center around eating, including the last supper Jesus had with his disciples. Significantly, Jesus sometimes is referred to as the Bread of Life, meant for all people.

A popular analogy comparing the world to a village of one hundred people vividly reminds us of the vast discrepancy between God's abundance and how it is distributed among God's people on earth. Currently the world's population is about 6 billion, 200 million—numbers beyond our ordinary comprehension. So reduce this to a village of one hundred people, with each person representing about 62 million people. There is enough food for everyone, but:

- Sixty people are always hungry, and twenty-six of these are severely undernourished.
- Sixteen people are hungry at least some of the time.
- Only twenty-four people always have enough to eat.[23]
- Seventy-five people have access to a source of safe water either in their homes or within a short distance. The other twenty-five do not; they must spend a large part of each day simply obtaining safe water. Most of the work of collecting water is done by women and girls.
- Sixty people have access to adequate sanitation—they have public or household sewage disposal—while forty do not.
- Sixty-eight breathe clean air, while thirty-two breathe polluted air.[24]

Second, the theme of hunger appears often as a reminder of the precariousness of life and the preciousness of God's gift of food. Famine is viewed as both a natural calamity (Genesis 12:1, 37-50) and as a consequence of sin.[25] Jacob's sons went down to the land of Pharaoh in search of grain, and eventually their descendants were enslaved in Egypt. Ruth left the land of Moab to glean surplus corn in the fields of Boaz. Because he was hungry, David stole sacred bread from the house of God. Robert Hutchinson notes that:

> Whenever prosperity led the people of Israel to forget their God and begin worshiping the things they had made with their own hands, the idols of gold and silver; whenever they forgot the desert and the Promise and the years of bondage in Egypt; whenever they neglected the poor, the alien, the widow, a famine or other natural disaster occurred and reminded them once again of their total dependence on the mysterious Power which rules the universe and which had led them forth from the land of Egypt.[26]

David Beckmann and Arthur Simon have pointed out, however, that "famines are just the tip of the iceberg, responsible for about 3 percent of the approximately seven million hunger-related deaths that occur in a typical year."[27] One biblical commentator notes that "rampant waste, astronomical military expenditures, exploitation of the goods of the earth, gross eating habits, and all the rest of the fundamental evils in the development of industrialized societies have to be identified as contributing to world famine."[28]

L. Shannon Jung suggests that the goodness of food represents the incarnation of Jesus Christ. He claims that "good food and delightful meals can remind us of the many ways God's grace becomes incarnate in our lives."[29]

Third, feeding the hungry is both a moral obligation and a religious requirement. The Hebrew prophets repeatedly emphasized feeding the poor. The prophet Isaiah thunders the requirements of God: "Is it not to share your bread with the hungry, and bring the homeless poor into your house?" (Isaiah 58:7).

Jewish traditions did not leave caring for the hungry to the chance of voluntary philanthropy. Legal codes were written to explicitly guarantee the protection of the poor. Every seventh year (or Jubilee Year) debts were to be forgiven (Deuteronomy 15:1-2). The hungry had a right to glean food left over in the fields from harvests, and owners were urged not to strip all produce from their fields, vineyards, or olive trees (Leviticus 19:9-10; Deuteronomy 24:19-21). Owners were instructed to give the hungry a tithe of all their crops every third year (Deuteronomy 14:28-29; 26:12).[30]

Jewish teaching always underscores the imperative of helping the hungry. The Talmud states, "Providing charity for poor and hungry people weighs as heavily as all the other commandments of the Torah combined" (*Baba Batra* 9a). The Midrash emphasizes that God says to Israel, "My children, whenever you give sustenance to the poor, I impute it to you as though you gave sustenance to Me." Does God eat and drink? "No, but whenever you give food to the poor, God accounts it to you as if you gave food to Him" (Midrash Tannaim). Rabbi Marc H. Tannenbaum summarizes the Jewish position this way:

> If one takes seriously the moral, spiritual, and humanitarian values of Biblical, Prophetic, and Rabbinic Judaism, the inescapable issue of conscience that must be faced is: How can anyone justify not becoming involved in trying to help save the lives of starving millions of human beings throughout the world whose plight constitutes the most agonizing moral and humanitarian problem?[31]

Emphasizing the importance of being compassionate with food, Jesus defended his disciples when they picked wheat on the Sabbath, against the establishing religious rules of the day. Citing Hosea, Jesus declared, "I desire mercy and not sacrifice" (Matthew 12:7; see Hosea 6:6).

Fourth, sharing is the essence of the spiritual life. The feeding miracles of Jesus—the multiplication of loaves—are reported in all four Gospels (Matthew 14:13-21; Mark 6:32-44; Luke 9:12-17; John 6:5-13). Some biblical commentators think the greatest miracle is that people generously shared their food. In unambiguous language, the writers of Matthew, Mark, and Luke record Jesus commanding the disciples, "You give them something to eat" (Matthew 14:16; Mark 6:37; Luke 9:13).

The early church emphasized the common sharing of food and collections for the hungry. The Book of Acts records that members of the early Jerusalem Christian community shared bread together and that selling houses and property in order to provide food for the needy was recommended (Acts 2:44-45; 4:34-35). These practices were so well-known that even Julian the Apostate, who wanted to restore polytheism to Rome, could not overlook Jewish and Christian acts of love. Urging his government to act charitably and justly, he wrote, "We ought to be ashamed. Not a beggar is to be found among the Jews, and those godless Galileans [the Christians] feed not only their own people but ours as well, whereas our people receive no assistance whatever from us."[32]

In his book *Ethics*, Dietrich Bonhoeffer declared, "To allow the hungry man to remain hungry would be blasphemy against God and one's neighbor, for what is nearest to God is precisely the need of one's neighbor." Sharing food is a witness to God's grace. Emphasizing that sharing is the essence of the spiritual life, Bonhoeffer wrote:

> It is for the love of Christ, which belongs as much to the hungry man as to myself, that I share my bread with him and that I share my dwelling with the homeless. If the hungry man does not attain to faith, then the fault falls on those who refused him bread. To provide the hungry man with bread is to prepare the way for the coming of grace.[33]

Fifth, failure to feed the hungry is deemed a serious sin. When Job was suffering, his friends thought his misfortune might have been caused by his misdeeds. Thus they declared, "You have given no water to the weary to drink, and you have withheld bread from the hungry" (Job 22:7). Job defends himself, saying he never failed to provide food for the widow and the orphan (Job 29:12-13).

Jesus provides only one explicit image of a person in "hell": that of the rich man, Lazarus, who lets a sick person starve at his doorstep

(Luke 16:19-31). John Hall Snow suggests, "To let people starve is, for Jesus, the ultimate sin."[34] In heaven the positions of the poor and the rich are reversed. Pope John Paul II used this metaphor in a homily delivered to eighty thousand people in New York's Yankee Stadium. He declared:

> All of humanity must think of the parable of the rich man and the beggar. Humanity must translate it into contemporary terms, in terms of economy and politics, in terms of all human rights, in terms of relations between the "first," "second" and "third world." We cannot stand idly by when thousands of human beings are dying of hunger.[35]

Sixth, both Jewish and Christian rituals emphasize the importance of sharing food. The holiest of Jewish holidays, Yom Kippur, involves fasting as a reminder of dependence upon God and the need to share with others.

Christians around the world recite the Lord's Prayer, saying, "Give us this day our daily bread." This prayer reminds us that food is a gift of God and not just the result of human efforts. Jesus' sharing in the Last Supper has become the sacrament of the Eucharist. This covenant of discipleship linked sharing food with the hungry to intimacy with God.[36] The apostle Paul thought that participation in the symbolic blood and body of Christ required serious self-examination (1 Corinthians 11:28-32).

Discipleship involves more than hoping people get food. The writer of James explicitly asks, "If a brother or sister is naked and lacks daily food, and one of you says to them, 'Go in peace; keep warm and eat your fill,' and yet you do not supply their bodily needs, what is the good of that?" (James 2:15-16). Faith without works is dead; hoping without helping is sinful.

Seventh, abolishing hunger on earth has always been a religious imperative. Though Christianity emerged in a time of gross social inequalities and the possibility of ending hunger seemed impossible, Christians have persistently claimed an eschatological vision of the kingdom of God when all God's people "will hunger no more, and thirst no more; . . . and God will wipe away every tear from their eyes" (Revelation 7:16-17). Jesus promised the poor they would inherit the kingdom of God: "Blessed are you who are hungry now; for you will be filled" (Luke 6:21). This vision over the centuries has motivated the church's mission and ministry to be involved in works of justice and acts of charity that have sought to conquer the forces of hunger.

Christian idealists and pragmatic politicians at times find common ground in words from Romans: "If your enemies are hungry, feed them; if they are thirsty, give them something to drink; for by doing this you will heap burning coals on their heads" (Romans 12:20). Abraham Lincoln once said, "Do I not conquer my enemy, by making him my friend?"[37]

Eighth, Christians of all theological persuasions—Protestant or Roman Catholic, conservative or liberal, Pentecostals or Presbyterians—believe that the cry of the hungry is actually the voice of God. Jesus made it abundantly clear that failing to feed the hungry was equivalent to not sharing food with him. "Truly I tell you, just as you did it to one of the least of these who are members of my family, you did it to me" (Matthew 25:40). God in Christ is incognito in the needy and the hungry.

In fact, at the Last Judgment Christians are not asked their theological perspectives on the Trinity, or whether they have been Republicans or Democrats, or even their viewpoints on many contemporary "hot button" ethical issues. Rather the questions focus on whether we have fed the hungry, given drink to the thirsty, clothed the naked, visited the sick, and cared for those in prison (Matthew 25:34-46).

The narrator of *The Journey*, a powerful oratorio by Nancy Telfer, speaks of listening to the agony of God. She notes how she, who has never been hungry for a day, sees children starving for bread. She, who is always warm, sees those who lack a sheltering home. She, who has always been strong, sees stunted children and yearns to make them whole. An excerpt reminds us of how the cry of the hungry can be the voice of God:

I listen to the agony of God—
But know full well
That not until I share their bitter cry—
earth's pain and hell—
can God within my spirit dwell
to bring the Kingdom nigh.[38]

From Apathy to Action

In light of biblical and theological teachings regarding the sin of selfishness and the will of God in feeding the hungry, why are not people of faith obsessed with ending world hunger now? What keeps us complacent and apathetic about the possibility of eliminating malnourishment and starvation? These are haunting questions that torment a sensitive spiritual soul.

L. Shannon Jung notes that we personally benefit from a degree of participation in the deadly sin of sloth. Our own complicity with the massive complexity of food production and consumption, our own desire to enjoy an incredibly high standard of living, and our own enmeshment in economic and political structures make it seem impossible to break our patterns of behavior when it comes to addressing global hunger. "Sloth," says Jung, "seduces us from compassionate action by cheapening God's grace and under-emphasizing our empowerment by God."[39] The danger, says theologian Craig L. Nessan, is that "our sloth steals from us any sense of urgency in responding to the needs of our hungry neighbors, replacing it with a sense of futility. We become indifferent, apathetic, spiritually dead."[40]

I remember years ago, when I was a student, I confronted face-to-face for the first time hungry children, who were among refugees in Hong Kong. A few days later I was shocked to see so many hungry Indian people crowded on the unsanitary streets of Calcutta and the train stations of Madras. A missionary told me that at first he was so upset being in the presence of hungry people that he could barely sleep. But even more disturbing was that he soon discovered that somehow he had grown so insensitive he could now sleep peacefully. Overwhelmed by the misery-go-round of poverty, hunger, disease, illiteracy, and unemployment, consciences become callused, and hope fades into helplessness.

Few deny the religious mandates to end hunger, but we take refuge in the fact that people disagree about the causes of hunger and the necessary strategies for ending it. We act like ending hunger is an ethical option rather than a moral obligation. We deceive ourselves by making up excuses why we cannot do more. We rationalize that "it is the responsibility of the government to act," or that "the poor deserve being hungry because they have so many children," or that "since the problem is so large, there is little, if anything, I can do." We excuse ourselves by praying for the hungry, even as we regularly eat excessively and consume far more than any of us really need. We seem totally ensnared by our chosen cultural standards of living and cannot escape the prisons of our affluence, the chains of obesity, and the handcuffs of self-indulgence. No wonder the early theologians described gluttony as well as sloth among the seven deadly sins. Literally, it brings death to those who have no food and prompts death for the most spiritual soul.

No greater irony or injustice exists than the disparity, both in the United States and globally, between the rich and the poor, the over-fed and the hungry. According to the World Health Organization, 1.1 billion people do not have enough calories to ward off hunger, while 1.1 billion or more of us eat excessively.[41] Sufficient food exists in the world, but overconsumption in the One-Third, or developed, world adds to the disparity of distribution. While the so-called advanced countries have only about one-third of the world's population, we consume about two-thirds of the world's food. Critics like Frances Moore Lappé note the high amount of grain fed to livestock in America, suggesting it is as much "as all the people in China and India eat in a year" and constitutes the "Great American Steak Religion."[42]

In order to get persons and communities of faith to mobilize political will and to act compassionately to end hunger, Craig L. Nessan presses several questions. How high must be the pile of statistics of hungry people? How high must be the pile of dead people? How high must be the pile of Bible verses? What will awaken the people of God from their comatose state?[43]

I believe God is calling persons of faith to join in the new world-wide movement to end hunger immediately. God has been at work in the world, prompting governmental and nongovernmental organizations to respond to human need. God has been speaking in the cries of the hungry and the poor, and increasingly persons and societies have been hearing and heeding. God has been seeking to unleash the "principalities and powers" of this earth to liberate people from the slavery of starvation and the hopelessness of hunger.

Much work needs to be done, as evidenced by the Niger famine in 2005 where severe food shortages threaten 3.6 million, especially the 800,000 children under the age of five. Clearly God is calling churches and others of faith to join in partnership in an common endeavor to rid the earth of hunger. For its part the church can do many things, as the following chapters illustrate in terms of advocacy and service. But, above all, it can make feeding the hungry an article of faith as important as any other doctrine. In classical theological language, it can make stopping hunger a priority matter of *status confessionis*, or confessional status: it becomes a defining mark of what it means to be a Christian and a plumb line for measuring the work of the church in the world. Not feeding the hungry and not working to end hunger in our time thus become a heresy equal to denying the Lordship of Jesus Christ. In Nessan's vision:

> The imperative to stop hunger transcends denominational divisions. The testimony of the Scriptures regarding God's defense of the poor and hungry is so strong that it belongs to the *sensu fidei* ("sense of faith") of the entire catholic church (cf. *Lumen Gentium* 12). The time has come for all churches to acknowledge both their biblical heritage and the scandal of hunger in the contemporary world. A kairotic ecumenical consensus could consolidate efforts to eliminate hunger in the 21st century. Such a shared *consensus fidelium* ("consensus of the faithful") of the ecumenical church would attain results far beyond any individual denominations.[44]

In this ecumenical spirit, this study book is offered to individuals and communities of faith in the hope of moving persons from apathy to action and from helplessness to hope. There is new urgency to the old challenge of feeding the hungry. Truly God is at work in the world; let us join with all persons of goodwill who are seeking to end hunger now.

Questions for Reflection

1. What do you think are the key new challenges facing the church and the world in ending hunger?

2. In your spiritual life, what most influences you to address the issue of global hunger?

3. What do you think of the idea that a Christian's failing to feed the hungry is heretical?

4. What is your reaction to making the ending of world hunger a matter of *status confessionis,* that is, making it a defining mark of what it means to be a Christian?

5. Do you see abolishing hunger as a religious imperative? Are you familiar with your own church body's hunger ministry?

Recommended Reading

For the most up-to-date information, including an interactive hunger map, which locates the world's hungriest people, see the Web site of the United Nations World Food Program, the world's largest humanitarian agency (www.wfp.org).

Beckmann, David, and Arthur Simon. *Grace at the Table: Ending Hunger in God's World.* New York: Paulist, 1999.

Messer, Donald E. *Breaking the Conspiracy of Silence: Christian Churches and the Global AIDS Crisis.* Minneapolis: Fortress Press, 2004.

Nessan, Craig L. *Give Us This Day: A Lutheran Proposal for Ending World Hunger.* Lutheran Voices. Minneapolis: Augsburg Fortress, 2003.

*Come, you that are blessed by my Father, inherit the kingdom
prepared for you from the foundation of the world; for I was
hungry and you gave me food, I was thirsty and you gave me
something to drink.*
    —Matthew 25:34-35

*We have the ability, we have the means, and we have the capac-
ity to eliminate hunger from the face of the earth. We need only
the will.*
    —President John F. Kennedy

2. Ending World Hunger: A Battle We Can Win

George McGovern

IN THE LATE AFTERNOON OF
September 3, 1944, a battered old German passenger liner that had
been captured and converted to an American troop carrier slid into
the harbor of Naples, Italy. As it did so, a swarm of Italian children strung out along the dock began to shout out excited pleas for
American candy bars and other rations. But before the U.S. service-
men on board could respond, the ship's control officer warned over

the loud speaker that nothing should be thrown from the ship. "This is wartime Italy," he said. "These children are near starvation, and in earlier dockings other youngsters have jumped into the water and drowned while struggling with each other for bits of food."

That was my first dramatic encounter with human hunger. I do recall as a boy growing up in depression-ridden South Dakota the constant stream of "hoboes" coming to our door and asking to be fed—sometimes volunteering to do work in payment. My Methodist minister father never rejected such pleas. After all, a central biblical injunction is to feed the hungry—including of course those who "hunger and thirst after righteousness." To my father, an offer by a man to earn his bread by the sweat of his brow was itself a step toward righteousness.

But even in the drought-ridden, depression-burdened days of my Dakota boyhood, I never saw real starvation. That was a term applied to "the starving Armenians" by our mothers reminding us to be grateful for our food and to clean our plates. One might also hear about starvation from missionaries returning from a year or two in Africa or China.

But in the war-ravaged Italy of World War II, where I was stationed as a bomber pilot in 1944–1945, I saw hunger every day. Sometimes after waking for an early bombing mission, my crew and I could hear young mothers scratching through our garbage dump in search of scraps of food for their children. And there were the constant pleas from yearning childish faces in the village near our base: "Hey, Joe—Hershey bar?" "Milky Way? Babe Ruth?" "Hey, Joe, ficky-fick my sister—five dollars?"

The Costs of Hunger

Those scenes of southern Italy's children in wartime have remained with me over the years. In 1997—a half century later—I was back in prosperous, wonderful Rome, the Eternal City, appointed by President Bill Clinton as Ambassador to the United Nations Agencies for Food and Agriculture. My mission was to give new force to the U.S. role and to the United Nations (U.N.) in combating hunger around the globe.

I did not see hunger in today's Italy or in neighboring France, Austria, and Switzerland. But I saw it in the carefully documented surveys of the United Nations agencies—the Food and Agriculture Organization (FAO), headed by a noted agricultural expert from Senegal, Jacques Diouf; the World Food Program, directed by a creative, compassionate American, Catherine Bertini; and the International Fund for Agricultural Development, under the direction of Fawzi Al-Sultan, an informed, no-nonsense Kuwaiti banker.

I have a special personal interest in the World Food Program because I was instrumental in launching it in 1962 during my service as director of U.S. Food for Peace. Bertini and her predecessors have led this international effort constructively and wisely into what one critic of the United Nations has described as "the way the U.N. should work after it is reformed." Diouf at the FAO and Al-Sultan at the IFAD are seeking a similarly dynamic role for their important agencies. Bertini recently has been replaced by a wonderful Christian layman from Indiana, James Morris. It has been my good fortune to become warm friends with Morris, Bertini, and Diouf.

These U.N. officials and their associates share a passionate belief that the presence of more than 800 million desperately hungry fellow humans in today's world is both outrageous and unnecessary. They have clearly documented the devastating human, economic, political, and moral costs of hunger—especially its costs in severely hindering, warping, and ultimately ruining the lives of children and their young mothers.

Today's malnourished pregnant and nursing mothers are producing tomorrow's barriers to personal, social, and economic development—malnourished, brain-dulled, listless children. Those fortunate enough to survive will drag through uncertain lives, permanently diminished, unable to be productive, happy human beings.

Rome has some of the world's best restaurants; its shops carry an abundance of fresh fruits, vegetables, meats, cheeses, and nourishing breads. Food, wine, and superb chefs are some of the delights of this majestic, historical treasure called Rome.

But when the U.N. technicians, experts, and officers based in Rome visit the U.N. field forces in Africa or Asia and such emergency disaster areas as Rwanda and North Korea, they see a painfully different world. Not only do they witness the gaunt faces and twisted bodies suffering the paralysis of malnutrition and hunger, but they also see parched or flooded fields, thin topsoil being blown or washed away, primitive farming methods, poor food processing, inadequate storage facilities, dysfunctional markets, and an archaic food distribution system. And everywhere is the shortage of sanitary water.

And they come back to Rome to file their reports and to wonder why such barriers to a decent, productive life can still be allowed in a world of astonishing scientific, technical, and economic capability.

The Conquerability of Hunger

Every expert in the United Nations complex in Rome knows that there is enough food, enough food-processing potential, and enough distribution know-how to end hunger in the world. Every one of them knows, whatever their moral and spiritual orientation, that all the religions of the earth command us to feed the hungry. Every informed person knows deep in his soul that there is no reason for a single child to cry herself to sleep from pangs of hunger. Every informed person knows that there is no reason for any farmer to see his hard labor wasted by mistaken water and soil management and the absence of a workable marketing and distribution system.

So why are so many of our fellow humans allowed to hunger and weaken not only their own lives but hamper the well-being of all of us in the global community that is our home?

I have been asking that question for a long time. That was the question that led President John Kennedy to name me in 1960 as the nation's first Food for Peace director, a post that enabled me to see firsthand the hungry areas of the world. We have made much progress since then. For example, in the early 1960s I presided over the shipment of several million tons of cereal grains to India annually to check hunger in that country. Today, thanks in considerable part to the food and agricultural development assistance of the United

States and the United Nations, including the Green Revolution led by our great Nobel laureate Norman Borlaug, India feeds itself and is a net exporter of cereal grains. The increasingly prosperous Indian industrial and commercial economy rests on this healthy agricultural foundation.

In the 1970s as a U.S. senator, I grappled with the problem of hunger and malnutrition among the underprivileged of the United States. The Senate's Select Committee on Nutrition and Human Needs, which I helped to create and then chaired in close cooperation with Senator Robert Dole of Kansas, led the way in increasing food availability to the needy by greatly enlarging the food stamp program and the school lunch program and launching the WIC program for needy pregnant and nursing mothers and their infants through the age of five. The committee also developed nutritional guidelines for all Americans that have been widely accepted. There is no doubt that remarkable progress in nutrition and agriculture has been made both at home and abroad in recent decades.

But the question persists: why 800 million hungry people, still? I went to Rome to represent the U.S. interest in answering that question because I believed the U.N. agencies have the answer—an answer that nearly all Americans will support if they are given the facts.

Ending human hunger is our most urgent task, and it is well within our grasp. Some global problems, including human conflict, intolerance, and bigotry, have no easy solutions. Hunger is not one of these insolubles. It can be resolved during a generation, and it should be made the first priority of the global community.

The Contributions of the United Nations

The United Nations agencies in Rome are working toward a target of eliminating hunger for half of the world's estimated 800 million hungry people by the year 2015. This is a practical goal. It should be achieved with a momentum that soon ends hunger for those still suffering after that halfway target is reached.

We cannot educate the minds of children until we fill their stomachs. We cannot adequately curb disease, mental retardation, and stifling lethargy until we have ended hunger. We cannot achieve productive workers and independent families and profitable trading partners until we produce well-nourished, functioning bodies and minds. We cannot win the battle against AIDS with bodies weakened by hunger.

Ending hunger requires two fundamental ingredients. In the short term we must underwrite the direct distribution of food to those currently hungry and starving because of the disruptions of war, internal upheaval, drought, floods, pestilence, or AIDS. Sudan, Rwanda, and North Korea are current examples of nationwide emergency hunger needs.

In the longer term technical, advisory, and financial assistance must be provided to strengthen agricultural production and food distribution and to improve the quality of rural life on the farms and in the villages where most of the people of the globe reside. We also need to strengthen and protect our forests, fisheries, land, water, and air.

This is not a task for Americans alone; it is the province of the United Nations, which, by coordinating the contributions of many countries, has a greater impact than a single country acting alone. But as the host country for the United Nations in New York and an important member of its food and agriculture arm in Rome, the United States has a responsibility and an opportunity that will serve our national interest and bless our souls: doing our share to end the blight of hunger that afflicts so many of our fellow humans.

Twenty-first-century Americans have a reputation for both being humane and responding in a common-sense, self-interested way to the needs of others. We benefited during our own early developing period by the help of more developed economies in the "old world." My fellow citizens can now take pride in the countless successes of the U. N. agencies around the globe they help to underwrite.

For example, the worst drought for many decades hit southern Africa in the early 1990s. Cereal production—the lifeline of the people—was cut in half. But the famine that could have killed millions was averted by timely warnings and prompt action by the FAO. Through its Global Information and Early Warning System undergirded by the marvelous

Earth Resources Observation Systems (EROS) based near Sioux Falls, South Dakota, the U.N. agencies saw the drought coming and swung into action with documented emergency requests to its member nations for help. The result: donor countries contributed three million tons of food aid and the logistical, coordinating, and distribution support to make it effective in preventing widespread starvation, especially among vulnerable women and children.

Meanwhile, scores of U.N. technicians are working quietly and unsung through the villages and rural areas of Africa and other developing regions to improve soil, water, and air conservation, to clean up polluted wells and water systems, to build farm-to-market roads, to instruct and assist pregnant and nursing mothers and their infants and children in nutrition, and to preserve and replenish forests and fisheries.

The terrible upheavals and conflicts in Rwanda, Burundi, Uganda, Zaire, and Tanzania that created millions of homeless refugees in recent years would have been vastly more catastrophic had it not been for the U.N. World Food Program. That agency rushed in three hundred thousand tons of food and saw to its proper distribution. Ultimately more than a million refugees retuned to Rwanda from other countries in what was described as a human wall on each side of the road. U.N. food and trained personnel were there to prevent mass chaos and starvation.

World Food Program specialists are now in North Korea overseeing the distribution of food—especially to children—and thus averting widespread starvation. The United States doesn't approve of the North Korean government, but as Catherine Bertini, former head of the World Food Program, puts it, "We can't turn our backs on a hungry five-year-old because we don't like his government."

In a very poor region of Ghana, in West Africa, reservoirs and irrigation canals built in the 1960s and 1970s had fallen into disrepair. Farmers could not grow enough food and had to seek work elsewhere during the six-month-long dry season. With a loan of $12.5 million, the U.N. Fund for Agricultural Development and its partners formed "water-users associations" to repair and maintain the water systems. Association members benefit directly because they grow high-value crops year-round, have more income, and keep their families together.

The Commitment of the United States

There are good reasons for the United States to press the United Nations to reform its methods of operation, including more clearly defined priorities, more effective and open administration, and better targeted application of food and technical assistance in the field. It is also clear that countries receiving food and agricultural aid from the United Nations must in some cases develop more responsible and effective means of using that aid to benefit the people whose lives the aid is trying to improve.

While recognizing these difficulties, however, I was embarrassed as an American patriot who once helped to liberate Europe from fascism when I was confronted daily in Rome by friends who wondered why the United States did not pay its dues to the United Nations. We then owed more than a billion dollars in back dues to the U.N. system, including the U.N. food and agriculture agencies in Rome. That is a lot of money, but it is less than the cost of a single B-2 Stealth bomber. It is the equivalent of $4 for each American—the price of a coffee break or a couple of packs of cigarettes. Paying the dues makes the United States a stronger partner in the battle against hunger, and it strengthens the U.N. peacekeeping mission and other U.N. activities, such as the World Health Organization.

As a key founding member of the United Nations, the United States will be more influential and effective in achieving desired reforms and a stronger U.N. system if our government acts as a fully paid up member in good standing. I don't like the image of Uncle Sam becoming Uncle Sucker, but neither do I want him to become Uncle Free-Loader.

As a longtime member of the U.S. House and Senate and during my service in Rome, I fought for our government to restore its support for the United Nations. I'm pleased to report that we won that important battle. I'm confident that our citizens are more than ready to continue paying $4 annually per person to keep the U.N. in the forefront of the battle to end human hunger and to promote the peace of the world.

The Creation of a Global School Lunch and WIC Program

In 1996 all the nations of the world gathered in Rome at the World Food Summit and committed themselves to reduce by one half the number of hungry people in the world by the year 2015. That commitment meant removing 400 million of the world's 800 million hungry people from the terrible plight of chronic hunger.

When I took up my post in Rome two years later as U.S. Ambassador to the U.N. Food and Agriculture Agencies, I learned that the reduction in the number of hungry people was not moving on schedule. The problem loomed so large as to seem overwhelming to my associates in Rome.

Indeed, the number of hungry people had gone up by several million since the 1996 summit. Faced with this discouraging situation, I proposed that the United Nations concentrate on two food assistance programs designed to reach 400 million by 2015.

The backbone of my proposal was a commitment by the United Nations to provide a good nutritious meal every day for the world's 300 million school-age children who were not now being fed. I proposed that we reach another 100 million people with a WIC-type program for needy pregnant and nursing mothers and their infants and children through the age of five.

Most of the advanced countries provide lunches to their schoolchildren. But in Asia, Africa, and Latin America an estimated 170 million school-age boys and girls receive no meals during school hours. Another 130 million school-age youngsters in these countries do not attend school and are condemned to lives of illiteracy. Most are girls, because of the favoritism toward males in much of the Two-Thirds World.

In the thirty developing countries where the United Nations has experimented with pilot school lunches, enrollments doubled within a year. As parents learn that the meager family food budget can be expanded by a least one good meal a day for their children, they quickly take steps to make sure that their sons and daughters are in school.

Children who used to be too lethargic to walk to the village school and then sit through six hours of instruction now eagerly look forward to the experience. Academic performance, enjoyment of learning, athletic ability, and overall health improve dramatically when empty stomachs are filled with nutritious meals.

U.N. studies in six developing countries reveal that illiterate girls have an average of six children each. These girls begin marriage as early as age eleven, twelve, or fourteen and may have five, six, or seven children before they are eighteen. In contrast, girls who go to school marry later, have more years between births, and have an average of 2.9 children. More mature, educated girls are also better equipped to rear their children.

When I was the director of Food for Peace, the dean of the University of Georgia told me that the American school lunch program had done more for the development of the Southern states than any other federal program. That good Georgia dean was the first individual to get me excited about school lunches in America and around the world. I'm still excited about this idea forty years later. I want nothing less than a good nutritious lunch every day for every child in the world. If we can reach that goal, we will literally transform life on our planet. I hope and pray that my U.N. colleagues in Rome and the governments at home will give reality to this dream.

This is something that we can do and that we ought to do because it is morally right. But it is also something that will benefit all of us in strengthening the health, stability, and productivity of our world. It will, as a welcome by-product, contribute to the income of hard-pressed farmers and ranchers around the world.

At a Group of Eight meeting in Japan, President Bill Clinton committed the United States to provide $300 million to school lunches abroad by asking Secretary of Agriculture Dan Glickman to purchase this amount of surplus farm produce for use overseas in school lunches. Other countries such as Canada, Australia, France, and Argentina could also contribute farm surpluses to the program.

Countries without food surpluses could contribute cash or transportation or administrative personnel. The United Nations World Food Program, with its experienced network of field workers in eighty countries, is the obvious agency to administer and supervise a global child-feeding program. No other institution has the trained personnel and the accepted multinational strength for this gigantic task. But other organizations can help. Many private voluntary organizations, such as Catholic Relief Services, Church World Service, Lutheran World Relief, the Mennonite Central Kitchen, the Joint Distribution Committee, the American Friends Service Committee, and CARE have operated for years all over the world. They know how to set up and, if necessary, run school lunch or breakfast programs, and they do it well with no corruption. This helps their members ensure a place in heaven. But it also ensures that the right food will be served in the right way with low overhead.

The American program WIC has been highly successful in reaching preschool-age children and pregnant and nursing mothers. Senator Dole and I, along with the late Senator Hubert Humphrey, were instrumental in starting it in the 1970s. I would like to see the United Nations adopt and direct this program worldwide. Along with the school lunch program, this could be managed through the schools with the help of voluntary agencies and local parent-teacher associations.

There are 100 million needy young mothers and preschool infants and children in the developing world. Added to the 300 million needy school-age children, that makes a total of 400 million. If we can reach the 1996 World Food Summit goal of halving the number of hungry people from 800 million to 400 million by the year 2015, we should then be able to wipe out hunger entirely by the year 2030.

This proposal caused considerable excitement both within the United Nations and also within the United States and its Congress. The proposal gained new force when my old Senate colleague, Bob Dole of Kansas, added his support and co-sponsorship. We now had the bipartisan commitment of two former presidential nominees of the nation's two major parties. We quickly gained the bipartisan endorsement of such respected senators as Dick Durbin of Illinois, Tom Daschle and Tim Johnson of South Dakota, Kent Conrad and Byron Dorgan of North Dakota, Pat Leahy of Vermont, Pat Roberts of Kansas, Elizabeth Dole of North Carolina, Ted Kennedy of Massachusetts, Hillary Clinton of New York, Richard Lugar of Indiana, Tom Harkin of Iowa, and others. In the U.S. House of Representatives, Congressman James McGovern of Massachusetts, a Democrat, led the way with the strong support of Congresswoman Jo Ann Emerson of Missouri, a Republican.

The measure was introduced and passed by the Congress with the support first of the Clinton Administration and then the Bush Administration under the title "The McGovern-Dole International Food for Education and Child Nutrition Act." President Clinton authorized the use of $300 million in surplus farm commodities to get the program started. Another $200 million has been authorized by Congress and the current administration.

The program is now functioning on a pilot basis in thirty-eight countries reaching 18 million children. What is needed, of course, is a much larger commitment of both commodities and cash by the U.N. members to reach all of the 300 million school-age children and the 100 million needy mothers and their infants and children through the age of five.

The full cost of reaching these 400 million children and their needy mothers would probably be around $38 billion a year—the cost of four B-2 bombers. The dividends from such an investment—improved health, improved learning, and gains in lifetime productivity—would be incalculable. Beyond this, I believe that a world free from hunger among its children and young mothers would be a world less likely to explode in terrorist outbreaks.

The Campaign for Economic and Social Justice

After world leaders at the 2005 Group of Eight summit promised to double aid to Africa to $50 billion, the popular rock star Bono, front man of the band U2, noted the decision could save hundreds of thousands of lives from hunger, poverty, malaria, and HIV/AIDS. Bono warned, however, that "It's not the end; it's the beginning of the end. A mountain has been climbed here only to reveal higher peaks behind it."[1] This reminds me of wartime words uttered by Winston Churchill in 1943, when he declared, "Now this is not the end. It is not even the beginning of the end. But it is perhaps the end of the beginning."

Climbing these political and humanitarian peaks to conquer poverty and hunger will require persistence and sustaining a political will. Now that I am eighty-three years old, I do not expect to see the end of world hunger—unless the good Lord extends my years beyond one hundred. But, as I noted in my book, *The Third Freedom: Ending Hunger in Our Time*,[2] I do intend to complain loudly to St. Peter if I am called above (or raise the devil, if I'm called below) before we end hunger in America. I also expect to see us reach well past "the end of the beginning" of our victory over world hunger. If we can now reach other planets thanks to the scientific genius of our space architects, there is no acceptable reason why this planet should still have millions of hungry and starving men, women, and children by the year 2030. Wherever I am in the world beyond, if such there be, when my fellow humans are finally emancipated from hunger, I'm going to lead a chorus of celebration: Hallelujah! Hallelujah!

To reach that day, we will require not only the help of scientists but also the grassroots participation of men and women in local water- and land-user associations, in the management of local irrigation districts, and in decisions as to how the resources of the great river basins are used. It was a group of scientists who staged the Green Revolution, but the food and agriculture revolution of the next three decades will triumph only if land and water management becomes everyone's business.

"Everyone's business" includes women equally with men. "Everyone" embraces the poor as well as the rich. The scientists and other experts who drafted the invaluable report *Crops and Drops* conclude, "There is no room in an efficient water [and land] management scheme for elitist roles for the wealthy or socially distinguished; often, the people who most need a new say in how water [and land are] managed, and who know most how [they] should be managed, are poor women smallholders." To that I offer a ringing amen. Gender and class equality in decision-making are essential to the victory over hunger.

A keener sense of social and economic justice across the whole spectrum of society in the developing countries is crucial to ending poverty and hunger. That sense of justice must empower poor people to shape their own destiny. Self-determination is the watchword of freedom and the path to a more just and equitable society. It is also the way to freedom from hunger.

It is significant that a whole series of careful FAO studies has shown that small landholders produce more food per acre than do larger landholders. Data coming recently from India, Pakistan, Bangladesh, Sri Lanka, and the Philippines demonstrates that small landholders are more careful and more efficient, apply fertilizer with greater care, and grow more diversified, higher-value crops with more reliance on their own labor rather than machinery. A recent FAO study found that small landowners produced more per acre in thirty-nine of fifty-five developing countries. In the other sixteen countries, the results were less conclusive, but the overall findings were a clear win for the efficiency of small family-type farming.

Long ago I concluded that the best and most efficient farmers in South Dakota and the nation lived and worked on family farms—meaning farms small enough to be cultivated by a single family while providing the family with most of its income. This tradition, which has made American farmers the envy of the world, was enshrined in the landmark Homestead Act in 1862 during the administration of President Abraham Lincoln. This act offered any settler 160 acres of public land if he or she were willing to live on the acreage and cultivate it. In that same year, two other agricultural landmarks—perhaps overshadowed by the Civil War—were achieved: the creation of the state land-grant colleges with their agricultural experiment stations, and the launching of the U.S. Department of Agriculture with full Cabinet status. The experience of all three of these great building blocks in the success of American agriculture should be offered to (not pushed or forced on) developing countries.

I urge the full involvement of farmers and their spouses in the management of land and water resources partly because I have watched such essentially political grassroots practices work so well in my state and across the land. Consider, for example, the Rural Electric Cooperatives launched in the 1930s. They enabled American farm families to band together in cooperative associations, elect their own leaders and managers, borrow federal funds at low interest rates, and then bring electrical power to the previously dark farms and homes of rural America. Almost without exception, those farmer-owned and farmer-operated cooperatives have been models of self-help and sound management, including nearly 100 percent repayment of the government loans and interest.

I have been flying airplanes since my nineteenth birthday. In early night flights over my home state and neighboring states, I saw a landscape that was black in all directions except for the towns and cities. From the air, the feeble light cast by kerosene lanterns in farmhouses and barns was not visible. And then came the Rural Electric Cooperatives. Soon South Dakota was lit from border to border with electric bulbs in the homes and barns and farmyards. A pilot crossing the state at night after that looked down on a sea of lights that illuminated the landscape. What could not be seen from the air were the electric-powered washing machines and dryers, the feed grinders and milking machines, the radio and television sets, the electric irons and refrigerators, the toasters and hair curlers—and everything else that heretofore was confined to the cities.

The farm families who developed and managed these wonderful electric cooperatives not only enriched their lives with low-cost electric power but also empowered themselves politically and economically by democratically taking charge of an important part of their lives. It is this kind of empowerment of the even poorer and more deprived people of the developing countries that must take place if they are to climb Jacob's ladder to salvation from hunger.

If American farmers can band together to light their farms— a task that large private utilities spurned because they believed it unprofitable—then similar farmer-run programs can work in managing water, land, irrigation, storage, reservoirs, and profitable public food markets in developing countries. The more democracy and equality of participation, the greater the chances for success.

The Two-Thirds world has more than its share of corrupt governments and ruling cliques that seek to exploit the people and resources of their countries. These governments are not interested in accountability or in open, transparent behavior. Thieving rulers who ride around in limousines to visit their posh estates at the public's expense don't want either auditors or an alert citizenry examining their behavior.

Thus it is especially important for people to develop their own grassroots management associations at the local level. Control at the community level of water and land, fisheries and forests is a key factor in all of this. It can be accomplished, but it will be a strenuous test of courage and political will. Victory in these matters must finally come if we are to end hunger in our time.

Perhaps the most promising activities for men and women organized in local associations are the child-feeding proposals made earlier in this chapter. I strongly believe that the nourishment of both school-age and preschool-age children, along with pregnant and nursing mothers, is the wisest action that can be taken in the developing world. It is the best way to encourage and underwrite education, which in turn leads to smaller, healthier families and more successful community development.

Preschool feeding programs and supplementary feeding and nutritional guidance for young mothers do not offer the in-place structures that schools can provide for their child-feeding programs. But if local associations were so inclined, it might be possible for young mothers, their infants, and preschool children to come to the school at a given time for supplementary feeding and nutritional counseling. Additional food, for the weekends and other meals, could be sent home with the mothers. Local associations might well devise alternative plans better suited to local conditions for these all-important preschool feedings.

The Crisis of International Aid and Trade

Of equal concern to farmers in the Two-Thirds world trying to succeed is the painful drop in economic assistance from more advanced countries. Funds for agricultural research, irrigation, and extension services have been severely cut back. There is no evidence yet that private capital will replace the reductions in foreign governmental assistance to these crucial farming enterprises. The cuts in such public investment are penny wise and pound foolish because they slow down the pace of rural development across the globe. That means less food and lower incomes for more than a billion people. Since this in turn means fewer customers who can afford to buy in the markets at home and abroad, everyone is hurt.

It is perhaps worth noting that according to recent public opinion polls, the American public has an exaggerated notion of our foreign aid budget, estimating it to be about 15 percent of total federal spending. When asked what percentage of the budget should go to foreign aid, Americans suggested an average of 10 percent. Actually, less than 1 percent of the federal budget goes to foreign aid worldwide. The military's portion of the budget is twenty-five times larger. The United States devotes just *eight-tenths* of 1 percent of its GNP (gross national product) to foreign aid, much less than Japan, Canada, Australia, and the countries of Europe. Also, much of American foreign aid is in the form of armaments to better-off countries rather than in the form of economic and technical assistance to poor countries. Worldwide, the combined annual total of aid to developing countries from advanced countries is $50 billion—a decline of 16 percent in the last decade despite the larger population of today's world.

The other side of the coin is that if the nations of the Two-Thirds world are assisted more substantially in the development of their agriculture, water, and other resources, they will not only eat better but be better customers for international trade. If they are then given a fair break in international commerce, with counsel and instruction from their more experienced peers in Washington, New York, London, Paris, Berlin, Rome, and Tokyo, all of us will gain.

It is the political and moral responsibility of the international community to make certain that the new global economy does not widen the gap between the few nations that are wealthy and the vast majority that are poor. If this happens, the street demonstrations that rocked Seattle and the World Trade Organization will erupt elsewhere around the globe. Anyone who does any measure of traveling and speaking at home or abroad knows that when the question-and-answer time begins, people will ask tough, sometimes hostile, questions: "Isn't the World Trade Organization in the hip pocket of the conglomerates?" "Who will hire me when I am fifty if my company pulls up stakes and heads for South America and cheap labor?" "What do these big multinational corporations with headquarters in Tokyo or New York care about the environment in India, or Brazil, or Attica, or Wisconsin?"

Doubtless, these questions about the newly emerging global economy will proliferate. But if the answers are honest and the actions of the World Trade Organization and the nations it comprises are decent and just, then humanity will have taken another important stride toward freedom from hunger.

The continued liberalization of trade is inevitable; few would suggest going back to the bad old days of high tariffs and other restrictions that isolated national economies from each other. At the same time, allowing a totally unregulated global market to run amok would let hundreds of millions of people fall through the cracks. The liberalized global economy has created great wealth for a few and has provided new benefits and reduced hunger for many, but it has also increased hunger, insecurity, and misery for many others.

Food security has tended to increase in countries that open their economies to trade and international finance and has tended to decline in countries that have not. Economic growth rates have tended to rise as countries take steps to be more competitive, and, though the benefits have not generally been evenly shared within these countries, hunger has tended to decrease as a result. A key variable is how evenly the benefits of trade are distributed within a country. Until there are means of ensuring a more equitable distribution, poverty and hunger among the citizenry as a whole are not likely to be much reduced.

Free trade is not a sacred ritual proclaimed from on high. Without a moral underpinning and a reasonable measure of public regulation, trade can degenerate into hot commercial greed, and the devil take the hindmost. In a brilliant discussion of these concerns while accepting the 2000 presidential nomination of the Green Party, Ralph Nader observed, "A society that has more justice needs less charity." Nader, whom I have long regarded as a national social conscience, added, "A just society is one that can better carry out the pursuit of happiness." It would be wonderful if the claims of justice could guide the emerging global economy.

Foreign direct investment has been very uneven: two-thirds of such investment in the developing world has gone to just eight countries, while more than half of all developing countries, including virtually all of sub-Saharan Africa, have received little or none. Trade as a percentage of gross domestic product has declined in nearly half of the nations of the Two-Thirds world. East and Southeast Asia's export-oriented growth can be given a large degree of credit for the dramatic reduction in chronic hunger in that part of the world; the increase in hunger in Africa is related, in part, to the lack of such growth. Since China liberalized its economic trade policy in the late 1970s, poverty rates have plummeted by 60 percent, and malnutrition has declined from 45 percent to 16 percent. Part of the credit can also be attributed to the move from large state-run farms to smaller family-run farms. It is important to note, however, that such economic benefits have been uneven, and many people remain chronically undernourished—189 million in China alone. More crucially, over the past twenty years, more than one hundred countries, with a population of more than 1.5 billion people, experienced a zero or negative per capita economic growth rate.

Only a small percentage of the more than $60 billion in food at retail prices exported yearly from the Two-Thirds world to the industrialized world profits the farmers producing the food. Rather, the money goes largely to the traders, processors, shippers, and marketers. For example, of every dollar spent by American consumers for cantaloupes grown in El Salvador, the farmer gets less than a penny. Only 14 percent of what Americans pay for bananas grown in more prosperous Costa Rica goes to that country's people and government; the rest ends up in the hands of corporations and absentee foreign owners.

Here is another rather remarkable example of how unevenly the benefits of world trade are distributed: the American basketball star Michael Jordan annually makes more money for endorsing Nike shoes than the combined income of all 22,000 Indonesian women who make the shoes. It is not surprising that many of these women are hungry, despite their day-long toils at the assembly line. I do not object to Jordan getting rich. He has for years brought pleasure into our lives with his matchless athletic skill. What is objectionable is the near-starvation wages paid Indonesian working women.

Brazil, Bolivia, Thailand, and Chile, all of which have greatly expanded their agricultural exports over the past several decades, have failed to meet the food needs of their population. In some cases the situation has actually worsened. This is not surprising. Those who control the food production processes will naturally want to sell to those who can afford to buy at the best prices. Given that traders in the Two-Thirds world can sell produce to industrialized nations at higher prices than their poor compatriots can afford, the market dictates that sellers should focus on exports. For example, although large numbers of Peruvians suffer from protein deficiencies, much of the fish caught in Peru's rich Pacific waters goes to North America for pet food. Why? Because American pet owners can pay higher prices to feed their dogs and cats than Peruvian parents can pay to feed their children.

Again, the issue of land tenure becomes critical. Both the Central American nation of Costa Rica and the African nation of Kenya place considerable emphasis on export crops. The average Costa Rican, however, has benefited far more than the average Kenyan because most of Kenya's exports are grown on large plantations owned by a handful of wealthy families, while Costa Rica's export crops are grown by many small farmers. Other factors include Costa Rica's stronger tradition of democracy, good government, and demilitarization, as well as greater support for education, health care, land reform, and social insurance. As long as governments fail to address such issues as inequality and corruption, no trade policy can meet the food needs of their population.

If export earnings were shared throughout a country's population, food security for everyone would be enhanced. However, often a poor country's foreign exchange earnings are used to import luxury items for the wealthy instead of food for the hungry.

Another problem is that the overall terms of trade in recent decades have been unfavorable to the poorer countries. Adjusted for inflation, export earnings for such raw materials as food crops, minerals, petroleum, coffee, tea, cocoa, and oilseeds have declined, while prices for finished goods, such as high-tech products and services, machinery, transportation equipment, and farm equipment, have gone up. In other words, it now takes a lot more bags of coffee to buy a tractor.

Unfortunately, the globalization of the economy has made it easier for corporations to move to places with lower corporate taxes, lower wages, and less restrictive environmental standards. Then there is the aforementioned incentive for developing nations to keep wages low so as to attract investment; this leads to situations like Indonesia's, where full-time assembly-line workers contracted by American corporations are often unable to afford basic foodstuffs for their families. In many nations of the Two-Thirds world, unions are suppressed, working conditions are terrible, hours are long, and wages often are insufficient to buy necessities.

Even in the United States, most poor people work full-time but still find it difficult to feed, clothe, and house their families. In South Dakota I have seen the farm families whose toil provides our food being forced to buy their own food with food stamps. I have also seen American soldiers shopping with food stamps to feed their families. Meanwhile, unemployment is at record levels in Europe, and real wages are declining throughout the industrialized world despite relative prosperity. The only way out of this "race to the bottom" is for nations to establish more humane minimal standards. Much of the United States' prosperity can be attributed to the imposition of federal standards at the turn of the last century. The federal laws made uniform the disparate state laws, which had provided little incentive to improve working conditions and promote overall economic development. Professor Stephen Zunes of the University of San Francisco has suggested that establishing global working standards for a global economy would be a major step toward promoting justice for workers and ending world hunger. This might be something for the World Trade Organization member nations to consider.

Virtually all nations recognize that government-administered economies are unworkable, that a market-based system is the way to go, and that their economic well-being is tied to being part of a globalized market system. But we must ensure that this dynamic system can meet the food security needs of all. This will require establishing some fair rules.

In summary, liberalized trade can increase economic growth through greater efficiency and comparative advantage. It tends to provide more choices and better quality for consumers at lower prices. It creates new jobs in poor countries. If the wage level were higher, it would be better not only for workers in poor countries but also for workers in advanced countries such as the United States. Cheap labor abroad drives down wages in the developed countries. That is a major reason why American workers fear free trade and globalization. If, on the other hand, wages and environmental standards in the developing countries were raised to a fair level, liberalized trade would then create greater interdependence, growing trust, greater cooperation, and the reduction of misunderstandings. It is quite possible to recognize the great advantages of open trade and the market system without falling into the free-market fundamentalism that ignores the positive role governments and international standards can also play.

Early in my career, I remember, South Korea, Taiwan, and even Japan were suffering from serious shortages of food; large segments of their populations were hungry. These countries were able to turn themselves around, providing plenty of food for their own people and becoming net exporters of food by temporarily limiting food imports while embarking on an ambitious program of land redistribution and subsidies for domestic farmers and businesses. The idea was that by increasing the income and purchasing power of broad segments of society, they could develop an adequate consumer market to support their local economy, at which point they could drop many of their subsidies and tariffs and compete internationally. Indeed, the United States' first secretary of the treasury, Alexander Hamilton, set up similar protectionist measures to allow our infant national economy to compete with more powerful European economic powers. But such a strategy, which other countries might want to emulate, is no longer possible under the WTO's new rules. In the long run, however, the answer is not protectionism, but a liberalization flexible enough to meet varying national conditions. Freer trade should not be seen as a goal in and of itself, but as a vehicle for human betterment that takes into account the benefits as well as the costs and modifies trade policies accordingly.

The continued emergence of a dynamic global economy, driven by trade and investment, seems to be a certainty. It can contribute significantly to ending human hunger, provided it has a human face sustained by a human heart. Free enterprise, yes, but free enterprise with a soul, even if that soul must sometimes come in the form of government regulation. It is sometimes argued that in the world of business and commercial trade, the only thing that matters is the bottom line. But let us hope that in the more enlightened precincts of commerce there is recognition of the wisdom propounded by Auguste Comte a century and a half ago: "Nothing at bottom is real except humanity."

The Contribution Each of Us Can Make

There are many commanding problems in the world, which probably all of us would like to see resolved. I suppose these would include militarism and war; racism, sexism, and other bigotry; environmental pollution; crime; alcoholism and other drug addictions; poverty; lack of family responsibility, including family planning; totalitarianism; illiteracy; and disease. It would be cause for universal rejoicing if we could somehow manage to resolve these problems in our time, by 2030.

But even confirmed optimists like me cannot honestly predict victory so soon over any of these long-standing curses of our civilization. I do believe deep in my soul, however, that we can and must end hunger in the world by 2030. I'm not referring to the temporary hunger that accompanies a war or civil conflict or to hunger caused by catastrophes of nature that cannot be foreseen. Rather, I write of the chronic hunger of nearly 800 million people, who bear this affliction throughout their miserable, short existence on earth. There is no excuse for this kind of massive lifelong torture, ending only with an agonizing early death. Yet this is the fate that has been dictated from cradle to grave for one out of every seven human beings on our planet.

No war in all of history has ever killed so many humans and spread so much suffering and disease in any year as world hunger now does annually. So if we cannot resolve *all* of humanity's problems, let us resolve to end at least *one* by the year 2030—human hunger. If we fail to do this, we will stand condemned before the bar of history. In that case, shame on you, and shame on me. If there is a scale of divine justice in the universe, we would deserve to choke on our food even as we listen to the cries of the starving.

I realize that as American ambassador to the U.N. agency responsible for much of what our nation does in the world of food and agriculture, I carried a heavier burden to discover salvation for the hungry than do my readers. But each of you can do something. Here are some possibilities:

1. Make sure your church or synagogue or mosque has an overseas arm as well as a domestic outreach that is feeding the hungry. Give money to these efforts, or to such philanthropic agencies as CARE, Bread for the World, UNICEF, America's Second Harvest, the World Food Program, and the Food and Agriculture Organization of the United Nations.

2. Stop complaining about the U.S. foreign aid budget, or at least that portion that feeds the hungry and helps farmers in the developing world produce better. Tell your representatives and senators to stop wasting money and lives shipping arms abroad and instead to do more to reduce human hunger. Foreign aid is a tiny part of our federal budget. Congress keeps cutting it. But if foreign aid is to be cut, let's reduce the destructive part—arms shipments—not the healing part—food to the hungry. The American Food for Peace

program of the 1950s and 1960s, which I have studied intensely, did more to keep countries from slipping into Communism and despair than all the costly military hardware we shipped around the world during the Cold War, much of it to dictators who denied rather than advanced freedom. And as we have seen, feeding the hungry abroad enriched our farmers here at home.

It is popular in some quarters to pan our State Department and its mission abroad. But let us not forget that the U.S. Foreign Service is widely respected as one of the best in the world. It is staffed by intensely patriotic Americans like us. It keeps a close eye on trouble spots developing around the globe. It works hard to strengthen American economic security and political objectives abroad, including the development of markets for our agricultural and industrial goods.

3. Become informed about the constructive work the United Nations does, and, when possible, refute some of the silly charges that are leveled at the United Nations by extremist groups. Let your friends and associates know about the work of such U.N. agencies as the Food and Agriculture Organization, the World Food Program, the International Fund for Agricultural Development, the U.N. Development Program, the World Health Organization, UNICEF, and other multilateral institutions, including the International Monetary Fund and the World Bank. Don't knock the United Nations. Recognize it as our best hope for international cooperation and peace, and a powerful tool in the battle against hunger, poverty, and disease.

4. When you encounter an American farmer, rancher, or dairy owner, tell her how much you appreciate the abundant food supply she makes available to us and to people around the world. Remind him of this truth: the American farmer is the most important person in the world. She keeps more people alive and healthy than any other individual. Ask him for his ideas on what could be done to end hunger abroad and in America. If there were an international Farmer Corps to assist farmers abroad, would she or some member of her family be willing to serve in such a Corps? Would *you* be willing to serve for six months or a year in such an international effort to reduce hunger?

5. If you should meet up with Bill Gates, Warren Buffet, Ted Turner (who has already generously given a billion dollars to the United Nations), or any other billionaire, ask him if he wouldn't like to ensure his place in heaven by investing a million or a billion in the triumph of humanity over the curse of hunger. He might say he is pursuing more important matters. If so, ask him to reduce his daily food intake to a crust of bread and a few spoonfuls of watery gruel for thirty days and then decide what is his most important interest and need.

Athletic coaches are adept at talking up the crucial importance of victory. The celebrated coach George Allen once told his players at halftime of a bitterly fought football game, "When you guys get back out on that field, just remember you've got thirty minutes to live. Either you die, or you seize the victory."

To paraphrase this superheated coaching rhetoric, we have twenty-five years to bring hope and health and life to those now facing starvation around the globe. It is clearly within our power to win the victory in that time. That means we've got twelve-and-a-half years until halftime, when 400 million of the world's 800 million hungry people should be eating adequately. We will then have twelve-and-a-half more years in the second half to seize life over death for the remaining 400 million.

The Charter for a World Free from Hunger

Doubtless there are other sound ideas for ending world hunger in addition to the ones I have outlined. But I am convinced that the charter or formula in the following nine-point summary can move the world to freedom from hunger by the year 2030.

1. A commitment by the President and Congress to end hunger in the United States. This could be accomplished by a modest increase in the minimum wage and an equally modest enlargement of the food stamp program.

2. An assurance to American farmers, ranchers, and dairy owners that if they continue to produce abundantly, the Secretary of Agriculture will be authorized by Congress to purchase a reasonable

portion of their surplus at a fair price for use in feeding the hungry at home and abroad.

3. The United Nations General Assembly should resolve that by January 1, 2030, there will be no chronically hungry people in the world. The 1996 World Food Summit in Rome attended by nearly every country unanimously agreed to reduce by one-half the 800 million hungry people in the world by the year 2015. The U.N. agencies in Rome have adopted this objective. Now we need to make a firm commitment to reach the remaining 400 million hungry by 2030. That should be the most celebrated day in human history.

4. America should continue to take the lead in working through the United Nations and the private voluntary agencies toward a universal school lunch program, embracing every child in the world. In pledging $300 million of surplus farm produce to this proposal at the G-8 conference in Japan, President Clinton took a large first step. Senator Richard Lugar followed up with hearings on the concept before the Senate committee on Agriculture, Nutrition, and Forestry. Former senator Bob Dole and I started off the hearings with a joint bipartisan appearance.

5. The United States should take the lead within the United Nations and the private voluntary agencies in establishing a daily feeding program for pregnant and nursing mothers and their preschool children through age five. This program would be patterned after the highly successful American WIC program.

6. The United Nations agencies in Rome should establish carefully monitored grain reserves around the world to meet crisis situations, including natural disasters.

7. The U.N. Food and Agriculture agencies must expand and improve their efforts to assist nations of the Two-Thirds world in strengthening their own production, processing, and distribution of food.

8. The United Nations should establish an international Farmer Corps patterned after the American Peace Corps but staffed largely by retired farmers and their spouses to teach farm families in developing countries how to improve their operations. American farmers and their spouses could play this role well.

9. The nations of the world should take full advantage of scientific agriculture, including the genetic modification of crops. Every scientific breakthrough in history has been greeted with controversy. Honest criticism should be given an honest answer. But there is little doubt that science can play an important and perhaps victorious role in the battle to achieve freedom from hunger.

There comes to mind a verse from the Hebrew Scriptures, by the ancient scribe Ecclesiastes: "For everything there is a season, and a time for every matter under heaven" (3:1). I believe this is the season when all God's children the world over should launch a triumphant campaign to banish hunger from the earth. Can there be any higher "matter under heaven"?

Questions for Reflection

1. What percentage of the federal U.S. budget should be allocated to foreign aid assistance? Why?

2. What should determine whether a country receives American assistance in feeding the hungry of their country?

3. What can be done to stimulate greater economic and social justice in the United States and the world?

4. Do you think liberalized free trade will increase or decrease hunger in the world? Why?

5. To achieve victory in the battle against hunger, what steps do you advocate?

Recommended Reading

McGovern, George. *The Essential Freedom: Our Founders and the Liberal Tradition.* New York: Simon & Schuster, 2004.

McGovern, George. *The Third Freedom: Ending Hunger in Our Time.* New York: Simon & Schuster, 2001.

. . . if you offer your food to the hungry and satisfy the needs of the afflicted, then your light shall rise in darkness and your gloom be like the noonday.
    —Isaiah 58:10

You can't build peace on empty stomachs.
    —Norman Borlaug, 1970 Nobel Peace Prize Laureate

3. A Commitment to Ending Global Hunger

Bob Dole

WHEN I BEGIN TO THINK OF THE daunting task before us, ending hunger now, I mentally divide this subject into the domestic effort and the international challenge.[1] Keeping both dimensions in mind simultaneously is imperative, if we are to be committed to ending global hunger. It is my hope that together as people of faith, through a variety of efforts, we can indeed formulate a strategy for ending hunger now. As my wife, United States Senator Elizabeth Dole, recently noted, "The battle to end hunger is a campaign that cannot be won in months, or even a few years, but it is a victory within reach."[2]

Starting with a Single Step

Like all great journeys, it must start with a single step. In this case, many steps have already been taken, going back to the White House Conference on Food, Nutrition, and Health in 1969. The first—and only—White House Conference on this issue, it represents the benchmark of federal policy in nutrition and health. Several landmark policies with profound and lasting impacts emerged from that conference, including the expansion of the food stamp program, food labeling, and the school lunch program.

There is a very proud history of bipartisanship in the war against hunger. Political strategists now divide the country into Republican red and Democratic blue states, but I believe with David Beckmann that "hunger is not a red issue or a blue issue, but a red, white, and blue issue."[3] President Dwight D. Eisenhower initially signed Public Law 480 that established the Food for Peace Program, and President John F. Kennedy appointed George McGovern the country's first Food for Peace director. It was President Richard Nixon who chaired the White House Conference on Food, Nutrition, and Health. I would remind us of what he said at the opening general session on December 2, 1969:

> Malnourishment is a national concern because we are a nation that cares about its people, how they feel, how they live. We care whether they are well and whether they are happy.
>
> First of all there is a moral imperative: Our national conscience requires it. We must because we can. We are the world's richest nation. We are the best-educated nation. We have an agricultural abundance that ranks as a miracle of the modern world. This Nation cannot long continue to live with its conscience if millions of its own people are unable to get an adequate diet.
>
> Even in purely practical terms there are compelling considerations for requiring this challenge to be met.
>
> A child ill-fed is dulled in curiosity, lower in stamina, distracted from learning.

Those words are as true today as they were in 1969.

Combating Hunger around the World

Further, President Nixon's words apply with equal force to children all around this increasingly small planet. A child ill-fed is, indeed, dulled in curiosity, lower in stamina, and distracted from learning. It is a scientific fact.

If we are to increase the standard of living around the world, we must increase worker productivity. If we are to increase worker productivity, we must improve the educational system here in the United States and throughout the world. And if we are going to prepare children to learn, we must feed them.

In short, feeding the children of the world is the correct thing to do and it is also the pragmatic thing to do. As productivity increases around the world, we will have more countries to trade with, and we will expand markets for the goods and services produced here in the United States. As hunger decreases around the world, the birth rate will decrease, and the standard of living will improve.

I am also confident that widespread hunger is one of the contributing factors that leads to discontent and creates an environment that is conducive to terrorism. We need to root out terrorist leaders and destroy the al-Qaeda network. In 2002 I advocated, along with Senator McGovern, that of the $40 billion authorized by Congress to fight terrorism, $5 billion should be earmarked over the next five years to reduce world hunger.[4] Better nutrition alone, of course, will not end terrorism, but we believed it could help dry up the swamplands of hunger and despair that serve as potential recruiting grounds for terrorists.

I concur with the congressman who introduced legislation supporting the Global Food for Education Initiative. he declared that in fighting terrorism we also must seek

> to eliminate poverty, hunger, ignorance and intolerance, which often breed despair, disaffection, and deep resentment. It is not enough to demonstrate what we are against. We need to be equally forceful in showing the world what we are for.[5]

Africa faces major challenges. Some 186 million Africans lack sufficient food, and 31 million African children are malnourished. Sustainable economic growth depends upon stimulating investment in agricultural production. Headlines from Africa are dominated by news of famines, wars, HIV/AIDS, and various childhood diseases. Therefore, I cochair the Partnership to Cut Hunger and Poverty in Africa with President Joaquim Chissano of Mozambique, President John Agyekum Kufuor of Ghana, former Indiana Congressman Lee Hamilton, and others. I believe with Presidents Chissano and Kufuor that "we cannot expect long-term stability, let alone sustainable democracy, in the face of widespread hunger and poverty."[6]

We have supported President George W. Bush's major new U.S. foreign aid strategy in that the Millennium Challenge Account makes foreign aid performance-based. Assistance flows to countries and areas where it can be demonstrated they are making a real difference to reduce poverty and end hunger. It should be noted that the African Presidents Chissano and Kufuor have proposed that the United States increase specific assistance in five vital areas:

(1) strengthening private enterprise by building on the African Growth and Opportunity Act to open global markets to African raw and processed agricultural products; (2) improving agricultural technology development and transfer, including biotechnology; (3) linking food and emergency aid to a longer-term development strategy, like the Food for Education Initiative promoted by former Sens. George McGovern and Bob Dole; (4) building capacity and institutions for education, research, policy deliberations and governance, including property rights and the rule of law; and (5) creating infrastructure for rural Africa.[7]

Combating hunger around the world must be a high-priority foreign policy objective as well as a matter of concern to all people of faith. The costs and consequences of failing to help feed the world's malnourished, especially the children, will have incalculable long-range personal and political impacts.

Addressing Hunger in the United States

On the domestic front, I think it is important to recognize the enormous progress we have made since the 1969 White House Conference on Food and Nutrition. In great part due to the leadership of George McGovern, there is a significant bipartisan commitment to eliminating hunger in the United States. In my farewell address to the United States Senate in 1996, I made special reference to how McGovern and I had collaborated closely together for many years on programs for low-income Americans related to nutrition, food stamps, school lunches, and supplemental food assistance for woman, infants, and children. Some even questioned how a political conservative like myself could even be a conservative if I worked with a political liberal like McGovern![8]

In the early 1970s, the United States sharply reduced hunger, partly by strengthening food assistance programs. But progress against hunger has not continued, and hunger has increased over the last several years. Millions of concerned people contribute time and money to charities that help hungry people, but private charity alone cannot end hunger. That's why a large majority of U.S. voters support efficient public programs that help hungry people become self-reliant and feed their own families.

All the national anti-hunger organizations have together developed a Blueprint to End Hunger. It outlines a strategy to cut U.S. hunger and food insecurity in half by 2010 and end hunger by 2015. The Blueprint is clear about the link between hunger and poverty; when families earn a decent income, they don't go hungry. But the Blueprint also stresses that our nation can make substantial progress against hunger by improving and strengthening the federal food assistance programs.[9]

Remember that American farmers are the greatest and most efficient food producers in the world. Yet hunger persists in the United States, with nearly 35 million Americans threatened yearly by food insecurity, including 13 million children. A Blueprint to End Hunger offers for consideration many practical suggestions for addressing hunger in the United States. It recommends that the federal government invest in and strengthen the national nutrition safety net so all eligible people receive needed food assistance. It advocates that public education stress the importance of preventing hunger and improving nutrition. This report also brings new attention to the complex issues of obesity in America and the unique nutritional needs of the elderly. The blueprint concludes by urging individuals to become involved with local anti-hunger organizations by donating time, money, or food.

Bread for the World has joined together with America's Second Harvest: The Nation's Food Bank Network, church bodies, MAZON: A Jewish Response to Hunger, and others in a campaign to *Make Hunger History*. It will mobilize leadership at the grassroots, local, and national levels. The campaign urges Congress and President Bush to approve legislation that will launch a national effort to cut U.S. hunger and food insecurity in half by 2010. The legislation will also strengthen grassroots groups across the country that want to improve the reach and effectiveness of the federal food assistance programs.

In 2002 the United States, through the Food and Nutrition Service at the Department of Agriculture, spent approximately $40 billion on the food stamp program, school lunch program, and WIC[10]—a major federal commitment!

Recently, as part of Food Stamp Reauthorization, Congress extended the benefits of the food stamp program to legal immigrants. The Bush Administration should be commended for its leadership on this issue.

In 2003, Congress reauthorized our nation's child nutrition programs. Agriculture Under-Secretary Eric Bost held a series of hearings throughout the country in 2002 to solicit ideas on how we can continue to improve these important programs. I urged the Administration and Congress to give close attention to a number of ideas that surfaced, including:

> increasing reimbursement rates in the school lunch and breakfast programs. It is my understanding that the current USDA reimbursement rate for a free lunch may not, in fact, be enough to cover the cost of the meal. If that is the case, we must examine the possibility of bumping up the federal reimbursement rate.

I also share the concern that many low income, working families cannot afford even the 40 cents per meal that is charged for a reduced price lunch. Perhaps that fee should be eliminated, thereby providing a free lunch to those whose family income is below 185% of the poverty line . . . , which is the guideline for WIC.[11]

These are important improvements that should be considered by Congress.

Advocating a Global School Lunch Program

On the international front, the McGovern-Dole International Food for Education and Child Nutrition program is just beginning to get off the ground. President Bill Clinton started the Global Food for Education Initiative as a pilot program in the closing days of his administration, using $300 million in discretionary funding.

The Global Food for Education Initiative now provides at least one nutritious meal each day to approximately 9 million children in thirty-eight countries. The pilot programs, carried out by U.S. private voluntary organizations and the World Food Program, has contributed to reducing the incidence of hunger in children, increasing educational opportunities, and attracting girls to attend school. The Global Food for Education Initiative is further strengthened when it is administered as part of an integrated development strategy for a particular nation or region of the world.

I favor a universal school lunch program for several reasons. First of all, from a purely humanitarian viewpoint, a universal school lunch program makes great sense for the United States. The greatest gift anyone can give is life, and we have it in our power not only to help 300 million children around the world survive but to give them a chance at a better life because of our kindness. 300 million: the tragic immensity of that number should sadden us all.

Another wonderful benefit of a universal school lunch program is that it helps get these millions of hungry and disadvantaged children to school. The promise of a meal—in many cases, the promise of life—will bring children to school who otherwise would not or could not attend, and once the educators have them, great things become possible.

If we choose to look at this problem from a U.S. agriculture point of view, then a universal school lunch program also makes great sense for our nation and our farmers. The United States leads the world as a farm surplus nation, and I can think of no better solution to that problem than to support a program that will help our farmers while putting food in the stomachs of desperately hungry and malnourished children.

For almost three decades now, I have worked with George McGovern and others on both sides of the political aisle to implement programs that help feed the disadvantaged of our country, while also giving them information on nutritional guidelines to better themselves and their families. Can we not work together to do some of the same things for the children of the world? A hot meal for a poor student today is key to helping him or her become a literate, self-reliant adult tomorrow. This could become the first generation in human history that is finally free from the scourge of hunger.[12]

My experiences in life have taught me that the generosity of the American people knows no bounds, and when they learn the scope of this problem, they will almost certainly want our nation to take a more active role.[13] The McGovern-Dole program was established as a permanent program in the Farm Security and Rural Investment Act of 2002 (Public Law 107-171, Section 3107), which was signed into law by President George Bush on May 13, 2002. That legislation provided for a mandatory $100 million from the Commodity Credit Corporation to serve as a bridge between President Clinton's pilot program initiated in December 2000 and the first allocation of the McGovern-Dole permanent program.

The goal is to get the federal appropriation back to a level of $300 million. We will have to work together toward this goal.

Clearly, the world community will have to build upon this program if we are to meet the goal of providing at least one nutritious school meal to the 300 million poorest children throughout the world. It is important to emphasize that if we are to be successful in ending hunger in our time, it must be an international effort. The United States cannot, and should not, shoulder this responsibility by itself.

Making a Difference

Ending hunger, domestically and internationally, requires personal and political will. Individuals, churches, and other faith-based groups, through study, research, conferences, and direct service to the hungry, contribute immensely to this effort. For example, I joined Senator George McGovern to speak at a conference on world hunger at the new McGovern Center for Public Service at Dakota Wesleyan University. That conference was an important part of building the political constituency for this effort. We need more such conferences across America to study and confront the issues of global and domestic hunger and how we can make a difference.

The Food Research and Action Center (www.frac.org) is a leading national organization working to improve public policies to eradicate hunger and malnutrition in the United States. A public interest law firm, FRAC is both nonprofit and nonpartisan. Throughout the years that I have worked with FRAC, I have found the organization a reliable source of timely information and research. More importantly, FRAC believes that everyone, whether Democrat or Republican, liberal or conservative, has a role to play in ending hunger and malnutrition in this country.[14]

I have united with President Clinton's former Chief of Staff, Congressman Leon Panetta, in asking people to join in Bread for the World's 2005 Offering of Letters campaign, *Making Hunger History*. You have an important role to play, too. Your letters to Congress make a difference. Members of Congress care about what you—their constituents—think. Together, we can get our richly blessed nation to recommit itself to make hunger history.[15]

Make no mistake. You can make a difference—each and every one of you. Even on great moral issues like ending hunger, there must be a political and social will that moves the leaders of both political parties to devote their time, energy, and political capital to such an endeavor. Like any important national issue, we must be able to explain why our campaign to end hunger should be a national priority. We must be able to justify designating precious and scarce resources to eradicating hunger around the world.

There is, of course, a federal budget deficit. How the federal government spends its money is a political process. It is a process that demands your attention. However, as a member of Bread for the World's board of directors and as honorary co-chair of the Alliance to End Hunger, I have visited President Bush and congressional leaders of both parties, asking them to renew our nation's commitment to ending hunger. Even in times of war and concern about the federal deficit, progress against hunger is feasible.[16]

We can accomplish the goal of ending hunger. We can elevate this issue in the national consciousness. This book is an important step in that ongoing national dialogue, and I commend people of faith for addressing this critical concern in our world. Working together, I'm confident we really can realize the goal to end hunger in our time.

Questions for Reflection

1. In what ways do you think hunger contributes to global terrorism?

2. How do you think the government should be involved in combating hunger in the United States and around the world?

3. Do you share Senator Dole's belief that we can end hunger in our time? Explain why or why not.

4. Do you share Senator Dole's optimistic view of the American people? If so, how do you see them encouraging our nation to take a more active role in ending hunger?

Recommended Reading

For more information about A Blueprint to End Hunger, check the Web site: www.bread.org/institute/blueprint_to_end_hunger.htm.

Bonanno, Alessandro, Lawrence Busch, William Friedland, Lourdes Goveia, and Enzo Mingione, eds. *From Columbus to ConAgra: The Globalization of Agriculture and Food.* Rural America series. Lawrence: University of Kansas Press, 1994.

Dole, Bob. *One Soldier's Story.* New York: HarperCollins Publishers, 2005.

For the LORD your God is God of gods and Lord of lords, the great God, mighty and awesome, who is not partial and takes no bribe, who executes justice for the orphan and the widow, and who loves the strangers, providing them food and clothing.
—Deuteronomy 10:17-18

This is the first generation in all of recorded history that can do something about the scourge of poverty. We have the means to do it. We can banish hunger from the face of the earth.
—Vice President Hubert H. Humphrey

4. Making Hunger History: A Trialogue

George McGovern, Bob Dole, and Donald E. Messer

HUNGER, MALNUTRITION, AND famine have haunted humanity for centuries. At the dawn of the twenty-first century, an estimated 850 million people daily suffer the pain and consequences of severe food insecurity. However, a growing consensus of political, economic, civic, and religious leaders now envision making hunger history.

In the preceding chapters, the three coauthors have shared their distinct perspectives on ending hunger now. Using a trialogue format, this chapter seeks to address questions people typically ask. McGovern, Dole, and Messer engage in a conversation on critical questions related to the quest of making hunger history. Topics are indicated by the subheadings, and each author is identified to clarify whose viewpoint is being shared.

Civility and Bipartisanship

Messer: Civility in public life and bipartisanship in politics sometimes seem increasingly rare in American life. Yet the two of you, Bob and George, as recognized national political leaders of the Republican and Democratic parties, respectively, seem to have discovered the gift of sharply disagreeing with each other on certain issues, yet working together closely on other questions such as world hunger. How has this happened, and why do you consider bipartisanship so important?

Dole: You know, I think we would both confess that in the early years, when we first came to Congress, we were highly partisan. I now look back at some of the things that I either did or said, and I was fairly partisan. But, of course, I like to think you can grow in the right sense. You do not have to change your philosophy, but you can recognize there are differences in different parts of the country. You might disagree with somebody who supports unions or who supports business. However, we have the same goals, and that is to make America the best spiritually and morally, economically and technologically—the best in every way.

Senator McGovern and I served on the Agriculture Committee, along with another great friend of mine, Senator Hubert Humphrey [Democrat from Minnesota and later Vice President]. We did a lot of things together, too. But it occurred to me, that watching Congress and what was happening, that when you had bipartisanship, the legislation was probably much better. It was going to be more acceptable to more people because it would reflect the views of liberals, conservatives, Democrats, and Republicans.

After I had been in the Senate for a while, I started reaching across the aisle. It was sort of natural for George and me. We both come from the Midwest. We had a lot of common interests in agriculture and the feeding programs, whether food stamps or WIC [Women, Infants, and Children] or international food programs. We started working together, and we got along very well. We did not always agree on every point and every bill that affected food legislation, but we worked it out. We have had a good relationship—we became friends.

McGovern: Yes, my cooperation with Bob Dole began when we were both United States senators, sitting side by side on the Committee on Agriculture. Previously I had dealt with hunger worldwide as President Kennedy's Food for Peace director.

I remember one night watching a CBS television report on hunger in the United States. At one point a reporter asked a young boy, maybe nine or ten years old, how it felt to be hungry. With a look as if he had kind of stubbed his toe a couple of times, he shocked me when he said he "was embarrassed." I thought, "This boy should not be embarrassed. Politicians like me should be the ones who are embarrassed. We live in the richest country in the world, and children are hungry." That prompted me to introduce legislation creating a new committee in the Senate, and Bob and I worked in a bipartisan fashion so no child should suffer hunger in the richest country in the world.

Dole: George left the Senate sometime after his run for the presidency. But I stayed on and became the leader of the Republicans, a post I held for about twelve years. I really understood then that strict partisanship is not the way to go. I think I had a reputation for being fair and reaching across party lines and trying to work out party differences. I think the most important legislative accomplishment, in addition to the different food programs, was working with Senator Patrick Moynihan [Democrat, New York] in 1983 to rescue Social Security, which was about to go down the drain. Once again I recognized the importance of bipartisanship and what it means to those in Congress and what it really means to the beneficiaries, the American people.

Messer: I heard you once quoted as saying that you learned from former Republican Senate Majority Leader Howard Baker of Tennessee "never to confuse civility with weakness nor generosity of spirit with surrender of principle."

Dole: Yes, I learned a lot from Howard Baker. We Republicans had not had the majority for a long, long time when he became majority leader. It was a new experience for many of us, to suddenly become committee chairs and realize we had power to set the agenda, making things happen or not happen. Howard had the right temperament and the right personality. I don't think he had an enemy in the Senate because he kept his word. Of all the things that you do not want to do is to violate others' trust in you. When you give a promise to somebody on the other side, or on your side, then you keep your promise. If you go back on your word in politics, and it's probably true in about everything else, your credibility drops like a rock.

Ending World Hunger

Messer: Working with the two of you in writing this book has certainly been a great honor and pleasure. I agree with Tom Brokaw when he called you leaders of America's "greatest generation." Both of you not only were decorated heroes of World War II and prominent political leaders, but also have been committed lifelong humanitarians. Some skeptics have suggested you only promoted food stamps and school lunches because it gained you votes in agricultural states eager to promote their products. Yet other politicians from farm states have not persistently pushed for similar programs, and once you left Congress you kept up the campaign to make hunger history. Why are you so committed to ending world hunger?

Dole: Well, I grew up in a family of very modest means. When I was county attorney in Russell County, Kansas, one of the jobs I had was to sign welfare payments every month to every welfare recipient in the county, three of whom were my grandparents, my grandfather on my mother's side and my grandmother and my grandfather on my father's side. So I knew a little about low-income America and how seniors had to struggle to make ends meet and how it is necessary to get certain federal assistance. It was called "Old-Age Assistance" in those days.

I also learned a lot in that office about poor families. I was forced to take children away from their parents, two or three times. So you really learn a lot at an early age, and it forms your opinions. I have never believed that everybody wanted to be on welfare, that these people are all lazy, and that if they just wanted to work they would not have any problems. Because, before you can accuse anyone of that, you first have to offer them a job. If there are not any jobs, you can get up and harangue all day long, but that just does not help anything.

When I was in my second term in Congress, President Lyndon B. Johnson sent me with several other members of Congress to India because they were having trouble storing their crops. Rats were eating their wheat, and a lot of people were starving and hungry, pretty much across the country. We went over there to make a survey and report back to the President. I can never forget how difficult it was to see these young kids with distended bellies and nothing to eat and no hope of anything better. That made a big impression on me, way back in the very early 1960s. So I think my background, my upbringing, and my experiences molded my character to a commitment to ending hunger everywhere.

McGovern: Both Bob and I have seen hunger close-up. We both were in Italy at the same time, a war-torn Italy of World War II, where we saw little children picking up scraps of food on the street. We saw their mothers rummaging through the garbage dumps looking for scraps of food. Sometimes you would see the same young mothers on the street selling themselves at night to American soldiers to pick up a few dollars to feed their families. So I think both of us carry those vivid memories.

Bob and I took that Senate Select Committee on Nutrition and Hunger Needs into some of the most heart-rending scenes of hunger in this country you can imagine. I remember going into a garage within a migrant labor camp in Florida. There we saw twelve children in that garage with an obviously over-stressed young mother with never enough food. She was trying her best to take care of these twelve children. Images like these in our minds drive us to do more.

Messer: I certainly understand the power of those experiences of meeting hungry people. All three of us encountered the tragedy of hunger in India in the early 1960s. My junior year abroad at Dakota Wesleyan University was spent in Madras, India. George, we first met when you came to south India as America's Food for Peace director.

People were starving in the streets of India. One could not walk to the train station without literally stepping over hungry children and their parents. Leprosy and hunger were twin disasters plaguing the people. Prior to the first shipment of food under the Food for Peace program, I had constantly been approached by poor children begging for a few cents in order to buy some food at lunch time. But after the food arrived, the children quit their begging and were able to return to school.

I will never forget visiting a hospital in central India where they were using milk powder distributed through Church World Service. Everything was used, including the containers in which it was shipped. They ushered me into a room where three premature babies were being kept alive in a makeshift incubator, constructed of the cardboard cartons in which the Food for Peace shipments had been sent. Up close and personal, I saw that international government food programs saved lives.

Now not only is India self-sustaining in food production, but it exports food to other parts of the world. Since the 1960s India's population has more than doubled to over one billion people, so truly the agricultural or green revolution is a modern miracle. Likewise I remember my mother saying, "Don, clean up your plate. People are starving in

China." But in the intervening years, China has drastically reduced hunger among its people. In 2005 China accepted its last gift of surplus food from the U.N. World Food Program because it now has enough capacity for feeding its more than a billion people. Another miracle in our time! Ending hunger is no longer a utopian dream, or even an impossible idea, but a high probability for humanity.

Strategies for Ending Hunger

Dole: You know, ending hunger in the United States is one thing we should not forget. There are still people in this country who do not have sufficient food, and a major cause is lack of educational opportunities. There are a lot of people in this country who speak another language. They do not know how to apply for the programs, although we have tried different outreach efforts to reach people in rural and urban areas. I think getting churches involved is a very important factor because they reach many, many people. Also we need to get service clubs like Rotary, Kiwanis, and Lions and many other civic organizations involved. They all do great and good things. It is going to take money, and it cannot all come from the federal government. It is going to take private initiative as well as money from state governments.

Likewise, when we get into international programs, America cannot do this alone. We are going to have to reach out to other countries, because the African countries where the threat of hunger and AIDS are the greatest are among those countries that do not have sufficient resources to help their people.

McGovern: The greatest cause of hunger is poverty in our world. Few people with a decent income are hungry. But, unfortunately, some 800 million, maybe as high as 850 million people now, are chronically hungry every day of their lives. They never have a decent meal. And poverty is the central question. That's aggravated now, of course, by this horrible tragedy of AIDS. It has killed hundreds of thousands of farmers. When hundreds of thousands of farmers die of a disease, their food supply is shortened, and families go hungry. When you have civil or ethnic conflict, those can be brutal things. War disrupts the production of crops and tears up the countryside. All of this contributes to aggravating the hunger problem.

In the United States we could help end hunger by doing two rather simple things. Number one, raise the minimum wage modestly. Second, increase the coverage of the food stamp program. Those two steps would just about wipe out hunger in the United States.

Abroad, we have to move on two fronts. We have to help farmers handle their land, water resources, seeds, and planting techniques in a more efficient way so that they can provide the major part of their food themselves. In the short term, we have to provide direct food assistance. We need to join with other countries in operating the school lunch program for every schoolchild in the world. We need to have a WIC-type program for needy pregnant mothers and their children for the first five or six years. Things of that kind help get food into the hands of people, who cannot wait until agricultural improvements eventually enable countries to feed themselves.

Messer: If we are to end hunger globally, I believe we also need to explore the ideas and plans set forth by the economist Jeffrey Sachs in his book *The End of Poverty.* He contends we could banish extreme poverty in our generation, yet we permit 8 million people to die each year because they are too poor and sick to survive. Sachs says every day we should read in our newspapers that "more than twenty thousand people perished yesterday of extreme poverty." Of course, we do not see such headlines, because impoverished people are nameless, and hungry people are hidden behind the glitter of globalization.

The World Bank projects that 1.1 billion people live in extreme poverty, defined as getting by with an income less than $1 per day. Sachs directs the U.N. Millennium Project, which has a goal of cutting the 1.1 billion in half by 2015. In his brilliant book he has mind-boggling statistics and big plans about how all of this can be achieved. Primarily he advocates five major development interventions: boosting agriculture, improving basic health, investing in education, giving people electrical power, and providing clean water and sanitation. Like the two of you, he offers hope to the world and a strategy for turning rhetoric into reality.

McGovern-Dole Legislation

Messer: Sometimes, however, people's eyes glaze over when they hear abstract statistics, big ideas, grand plans, and long-range goals about ending hunger, like those advocated by Jeffrey Sachs and others. On the other hand, people in faith communities and wider society can relate to specific concrete ideas like a universal school lunch program or a way to reach out to women, children, and infants in need. The genius of your approach, as epitomized in the McGovern-Dole International Food for Education and Child Nutrition Program, is that people can understand and appreciate how it might work. In particular, people can imagine how it would help support education, child development, and food security for some of the world's poorest children. What are your hopes and dreams for this approach?

Dole: Well, we are making some headway. I credit President Bill Clinton for getting it started, and President George W. Bush for continuing it. We do not have enough money. And we could never appropriate enough money in the United States to take care of 300 million children around the world. So, again, we need to make it a United Nations project. George was a leader of this when he was in Rome, as the U.S. ambassador to the U.N. agricultural organization.

It is probably not a kind thing to say, but I think some of the leaders in the developing countries do not pay much attention to the very poor people in their country. They must figure that the poor will always be poor and they should not spend any resources on them. At the same time that leader may have four or five homes across the country and a jet airplane and everything else.

What is needed is a lot of education and some constructive criticism. Our government might do it, but better by a consortium of governments. And then you get into the question of the very sensitive issue of birth control. But I think everything has to be on the table. We know the United States cannot feed 300 million. But we know we can do much better than we are doing. We have allies like my wife, Elizabeth, and Senator Hillary Clinton [Democrat of New York] working together on the Senate side, plus Congressman Jim McGovern [Democrat of Massachusetts] and Congresswoman Jo Ann Emerson [Republican of Missouri] on the House side. So we have some good allies. But we can do more. Our country can do more. But I think we need to keep reaching out and reminding other countries to help. I am not certain that is being done. Senator McGovern might have a better fix on that than I do.

McGovern: In 1996 all the countries of the world gathered in Rome and committed themselves to cut in half the number of hungry people in the world by the year 2015. That is now only ten years away, and we are not moving quickly enough to achieve that commitment.

How are we going to get 400 million people off those hunger roles in the next ten to fifteen years? It occurred to me that the best way to do it is to begin with the village school. We have 300 million school-age kids who are not now being fed anything during the school day. About 130,000 of those do not go to school, mostly girls. But when you start a school lunch program, the girls and boys come. Nobody has found a magnet as powerful as food to get poor kids into the classroom. Once that happens, both the girls and the boys show up. Their academic performance improves when they have a full stomach. Their overall health improves.

Another interesting thing happens. Illiterate girls, who stay at home without education, start getting married at the age of ten, eleven, or twelve. Unbelievable! These little girls! And they have six children, on the average. The ones who go to school, even if it is just the first six elementary years, marry later in life. It is not as easy for boys and men to push them around. They have a better sense of what life is all about. They have an average of only 2.9 children. So, on the strength of the school lunch program that gets the kids into school, you also tend to cut the birthrate in half.

Messer: Also, it has an impact on combating global HIV/AIDS, because young people, especially girls, who get an education defer their first sexual experiences and therefore reduce the possibility of becoming infected with the virus. By addressing hunger, we are also reducing the likelihood of disease and early death. This is yet another dimension of the value of the McGovern-Dole legislative approach to ending hunger.

McGovern: Absolutely. Another thing I have encouraged is that, when there is a school lunch program like this, we should try to buy a significant part of that lunch from the local farmers. Buy the fruits, vegetables, dairy products, meat products, nuts, anything we can buy. That helps the farmers as well as feeds their children.

Additionally, we ought to encourage the teachers and the children to grow a garden around the school. Get some primitive implements and dig up the soil and plant carrots, beans, peas, corn, and all the rest. There should be a garden around every schoolhouse in the world. That would be very helpful. It would be a way to get fresh, nutritious food. At the same time, it would teach the children how to plant food, something that would be useful to them the rest of their lives.

There is more to do if we are to reach these 400 million hungry people. The school lunch program would reach 300 million, and it will probably take ten years to accomplish getting programs going all over the world. Second, the world needs a preschool program that reaches pregnant and nursing mothers, which in the United States we call WIC for Women, Infants, and Children. Bob and I are the authors of that program along with the late Hubert Humphrey. It is a wonderful program, and we ought to do that worldwide. This would reach another 100 million, maybe 150 million, preschoolers and their young mothers.

That meets half the goal of feeding 800 million. I think we can do these things. We dare not talk in vague terms, "Well, we're going to cut hunger in half in the next ten years." How do you get your mind around that? I think the school lunch idea and the WIC program are something specific that everybody can understand. Certainly all Americans understand it. Other countries understand it. Definitely this is a program that ought to be under the jurisdiction of the United Nations but with the United States taking the lead.

Dole: It is going to take time. In Congress, you may not get your bill passed the first year, the second year, the third year. Maybe on the tenth year you might hit a double or a triple or a home run!

Messer: Bob, speaking of taking time to get legislation passed, I once heard you talk about how long it took to get the Americans with Disabilities Act of 1990 passed. As I recall, it took a long time before you were able to pass that landmark legislation.

Dole: We tried and we tried and we tried. Again, when we came down to getting it done, it was bipartisanship: Democrats, Republicans, liberals, conservatives, and a Republican in the White House (the senior George Bush). It was one of the greatest sights I have ever seen on the White House lawn. People came with their white canes or in a wheelchair or on a gurney. I think there were three thousand people there for the signing. And it was a sight to behold. The legislation stuck together because it was bipartisan.

Surplus Agricultural Commodities

Messer: Critics and skeptics question whether programs like the McGovern-Dole initiative are too dependent on surplus agricultural commodities and therefore not sustainable. How do you respond?

Dole: Well, I think that is a consideration. We have plenty of storage space in America. And we restrain the farmer from producing what he or she can probably produce. The family farmers are getting fewer and fewer. I think one farmer now can produce what eight farmers produced ten or twenty years ago. I think that is probably a fair question, but I do not think it is particularly valid. I do not think that would happen. We have these huge elevators where you can store grain, so we are not going to run out in this country.

Messer: But does it make other countries too dependent on the United States and reduce incentives for other countries to produce their own food?

Dole: Yes, it might make them too dependent. Another thing we have to watch, too, is that we do not want to disrupt their market, say by pouring wheat into a country. If they are trying to improve their economic viability with open markets, if they are raising a crop, we do not want to be competitive. That is yet another factor.

We have to make it clear that the United States certainly wants to be a principal player in ending hunger in our time. But we cannot do it alone, and we should not do it alone. There are a lot of reasons, not just because of the cost, but because you are going to have a better solution if there are more countries involved. You get more perspectives, and other countries may be better prepared than we are in certain parts of the globe.

McGovern: There's some truth in the criticism that the McGovern-Dole initiative might be too dependent on surplus agricultural commodities, and thus not sustainable. The critics are not entirely wrong. That is why I say we ought to have a garden growing around every village school. That is why I say we ought to purchase some of the commodities from local farmers. For example, we cannot ship fresh fruit and fresh vegetables all over the world. People should buy it in local markets. And that is one way to avoid the trap of making this program dependent on the availability of food surpluses in countries like the United States, Canada, Argentina, Australia, and other food surplus areas.

Genetically Engineered Food

Messer: Controversies abound regarding the causes of hunger and even the means of overcoming it. It is beyond the scope of our book to probe all these issues, but they are serious challenges that must be addressed by those involved in ending hunger. Chief among them is the issue of genetically engineered foods.

Millions of Americans, Canadians, Australians, Argentines, and others have been eating these foods for more than a decade. Critics, however, claim that biotech foods are unsafe and threaten future food supplies. Anti-genetic food activists even persuaded some African governments facing famines in 2002 to return tons of World Food Program corn because it was produced in America using biotechnology. Resistance to using these foods is particularly strong in countries related to the European Union and by other activists concerned about issues of health, environment, trade, and so forth.

The dilemma, however, is that the probability of ending hunger in the near future without developing, promoting, and using genetically engineered foods is highly problematic. Biotech food appears to be an indispensable tool in meeting the world's daily needs for food. The United States Ambassador to the Vatican, Jim Nicholson, even has argued that "sharing the fruits of biotechnology with those who hunger is a moral imperative."

Senators, do you think world hunger can be eliminated without supporting genetically engineered food? Do you believe the opponents of genetic agriculture offer any realistic alternatives to feeding the hungry?

Dole: Don, I think a lot of it is political. As you said, we have been using genetically engineered food in several countries—the United States, Canada, and Australia—for ten, fifteen years. Maybe it has already been done, but there ought to be some way to bring agriculture ministers to this country or somewhere in Europe and try to convince them it is safe and effective.

Obviously, we do not want to give anybody anything, or at a reduced cost, that is going to cause a health problem. And again, it takes time for something like this to happen—I was going to say, to wear down the opposition—but to put it in a positive way, to educate the people about the benefits.

I do not think we can make hunger history in the foreseeable future if we do not support and share genetically engineered food. But I do not understand some of the opposition, where the president of a country may have people starving, but refuses to let us give them genetically engineered food. It seems to be short-sighted and insensitive.

McGovern: We want to be careful about genetically modified foods. On the other hand, we certainly do not want to rule out the application of science to the production of food. Look what hybrid seed corn has done for the Midwest and for other countries. Norman Borlaug, the great Nobel prize-winning expert on food production and author of the Green Revolution, is a strong advocate of genetically modified foods because he thinks it is a good, clean, safe way to expand nutritious foods in the world, and I agree with him.

I think we ought to do testing from time to time, and we ought to apply the best brains we have to be sure we don't get into unnecessary difficulties with genetically modified foods. But most of the food in our supermarkets right now is genetically modified already. I have not heard of anybody losing a leg or a brain or their eyesight or anything else because of these genetically modified foods. I do not think it is an exaggeration to say that three-fourths of all the food on the American supermarket shelf is genetically modified. We ought to share our knowledge with the rest of the world.

Messer: So, am I hearing you say that we cannot feed the hungry without using genetically modified food in some way or other?

McGovern: That's my feeling. We might be able to do it, but it would be at much greater cost and much greater difficulty and a much longer time before we achieved it. Let me give you the case of yellow rice—golden rice, as it's called. White rice, which most of the people of the world eat, is short on vitamin A. It is short on iron and on other essential food components. Scientists operating in Switzerland and Germany have developed golden rice, which has plenty of vitamin A. You are not going to go blind eating golden rice. You may go blind if you eat white rice only. You are not going to suffer from shortages of iron or other food nutrients if you eat golden rice. Genetically modified rice is a wonderful breakthrough.

The Threat of International Terrorism

Messer: Especially since the events of September 11, 2001, the threat of terrorism has shaped much political thought and action. Most attention has focused on increasing national security, identifying potential terrorists, engaging in military campaigns in Afghanistan and Iraq, and expending dollars in countless ways to make Americans, in particular, feel safer.

I was interested, therefore, to discover that at one point the two of you suggested that President George W. Bush should consider using $5 billion of the first $40 billion allocated by Congress in an effort to end hunger. How do you see the challenge of international terrorism, including agroterrorism, relating to food security?

McGovern: I have always felt that terrorism is fed, in part, by the frustration and anger—and the sadness—of not having enough to eat, not having a decent house, not having sanitary water. In my opinion the more we concentrate on getting at the causes of terrorism, the better off we are going to be. And one of those causes is certainly grinding hunger, which afflicts so many people around the globe.

Dole: That is a good point. However, we cannot lay everything at the feet of poverty. There are a lot of poor people who, instead of becoming terrorists, have been great success stories in every country in the world, once these persons have an opportunity and equal human rights.

See what is happening in Iraq. They are going after oil on the theory that it will damage the country's economic progress, or prevent any progress. I assume that if Iraq had any big food supplies, they would be going after that too. Thus we have to be careful. We have to protect food supplies not only in Iraq but also in the United States and elsewhere. Terrorists are not going to go out into a field and start pulling up the wheat crop when they can go to an elevator, storage center, or warehouse and destroy the grain or the cattle or whatever. It is yet another thing we put on the list when we start talking about ports and railroads and airlines. Terrorists can poison the food, and they can do a lot of things that would make it unsafe. We have to understand that this is a threat. It may not be on the top of their list, but it would really cause havoc if they were able to destroy the food supply in any part of the world.

The Threat of Global HIV/AIDS

Messer: Every week the global HIV/AIDS pandemic kills more people than the terrorists who attacked the World Trade Center and the Pentagon. Worldwide more than 42 million people are infected, and more than 20 million have already died. South Africa alone has lost 20 percent of its farmers to the disease in the last five years, with another 20 percent likely to die by 2020. Malnutrition and food insecurity weaken people's immune systems, making them more susceptible to HIV infection and the onset of AIDS. Increasingly it is evident that lack of food and hunger are closely related to the HIV crisis.

Dole: No doubt about it. If you look at the HIV/AIDS cases on television from around the world, you will note they are generally the poorest of the poor. That may not be true in every case, because obviously it spreads from rich to poor and vice versa. But again, if we're going to lift people out of poverty and give them opportunities, they have to have food.

We have learned that, if you give young children in particular a chance to have a meal, more young people will go to school. In school they are likely to learn about the danger of AIDS. The churches and other faith communities in those countries need to be involved, too, in educating and teaching the young people. Young girls are apparently overlooked, particularly in some African countries. The males have priority; they go to school, and they get the food. Too often the girls start marrying at age twelve. Without education this is not going to change very much, so education is very essential.

Messer: Yes, the global school lunch program the two of you are advocating could affect the global HIV/AIDS pandemic. By creating incentives for children to attend school, you would provide opportunities for educational programs aimed at prevention, care, and overcoming stigmatization and discrimination.

Dole: Certainly they are not going to get any AIDS information if they are not attending some forum where they can get an education, where they can learn about the dangers and be told about abstinence or whatever program that might be available.

McGovern: AIDS is a terrible menace. I do not know what the answer is other than to try to convince young men around the world to use condoms. If they don't, they are going to spread any infection they have to their female partners, or they are going to pick up something from the infected women. We know that condoms will work. They do not interfere with sexual pleasure, and they provide safer sexual relationships. We have got to encourage that! I know that some people say abstinence is the best cure. Well, good luck!

Human beings have been having sex with each other ever since Adam and Eve, and you can't shut it down. Freud says it's the most powerful of all human drives. So the best thing to do is recognize that young people *are* going to be sexually active and to try to educate them on the importance of engaging in protected sex, rather than this recklessness when they don't use any protective devices.

Messer: The credo of public health prevention activists worldwide has been labeled "ABC" for Abstinence, Being faithful, and Condoms. Sometimes I think the C stands for controversy, however, since few persons in the political and religious community are as candid as you, George. You would have appreciated the poster I saw in Great Britain at the start of the war in Iraq. It featured condoms and read: "Weapons of Mass Protection"! It also noted that every six seconds someone in the world is infected with HIV.

How People of Faith Should Respond

McGovern: Combating hunger is critical to dealing with AIDS and terrorism as well as other global threats. People of faith should accept the challenge of eliminating hunger both in the United States and throughout the world.

I do not think you can be a Christian, Jew, Muslim, or Buddhist and ignore hunger. Every one of those religions demands its adherents to feed the hungry. Jesus says, "Inasmuch as you have done it unto one of the least of these, you have done it unto me." That is the way Christians serve the Lord. In this regard, there is nothing original about this for any of us. We three are all Christians. We simply believe there is a spiritual and moral responsibility to feed the hungry.

Every church member, every synagogue member, every Muslim, every Buddhist ought to make sure that their faith community has an overseas arm and a domestic arm that reach out to the hungry. My father—a Wesleyan Methodist minister, very conservative—believed implicitly that we are obligated to feed the hungry. In those dark Depression days growing up in South Dakota, I never remember my father turning down a hungry person who knocked on our door and asked for food. Those young men riding the rails West were looking for jobs. That was drilled into me.

You know, we would enjoy our own food better if we knew that everybody else had more. How can you sit at a gourmet restaurant and spend $25 for a meal and enjoy it, knowing that right outside in the street there are people who cannot make ends meet? So, Christians and Jews and other people of faith have a moral and spiritual obligation to deal with this problem of hunger.

Dole: Yes, all three of us are United Methodists, but feeding the hungry applies to all faiths—Protestants and Catholics, Jews and Muslims. Everybody can participate, and the more people who participate in making hunger history, the better off the world is going to be.

Certainly the church is a great incubator. The church can start to educate people—business leaders, housewives, and all kinds of people who have contacts with others every day. We need to spread the word about how to conquer hunger. I always thought in my political career that I would rather have a hundred people out there saying, "Bob Dole has done something good," than an ad on television knocking my opponent.

Messer: Bob, you have demonstrated remarkable political success and made a great contribution to America. If you were to have any fear about what is going to happen to the effort to feed the hungry in the world, what would that fear be?

Dole: Apathy. I mean, some people look at it and say, "It's just too big. We cannot solve it, so let's not do anything. These young people are going to die. There are other priorities we have to deal with." I do not subscribe to that. I do not think President Bush subscribes to that. I am almost certain he does not. But Senator McGovern and I hope to encourage him to do even more with reference to our program. Not because our name is on it. That is not even relevant. It is because people are starving; young babies and young children are growing up without an education. They are turning to crime, and they are turning to terrorism.

Messer: Both of you could be enjoying a quiet retirement. But here we are in 2005 and you both have been out of the Senate for a long time, yet you are as active as ever.

Dole: George and I look ahead. Let's say we have four or five good years left, so our goal is just to keep prodding the people who can make these changes happen.

McGovern: Well, I work as hard as I ever did. I expect someday just to drop in my tracks, working at some useful task. I think it was Harry Emerson Fosdick who defined happiness some years ago as being engaged in some useful task that benefited others. That is the only way I can do it. I cannot be happy just going out and making money. I wish I had a lot of money. There are a lot of things I could do with it. But I would not be happy doing nothing but making money. Now there's nothing wrong with making money, if you give away some of it to the poor and the sick. But I get my satisfaction out of things like working for the universal school lunch program.

Messer: Senators, I appreciate your lifetime of commitment and involvement in making hunger history. What motivated you to envision a book that was particularly addressed to people of faith?

McGovern: Because I think if we can get the churches and the synagogues and the mosques behind this effort, it will go. I think we ought to press our churches to make sure they have a good world-service arm and a good domestic philanthropic arm that address hunger. That is why I thought that a book of this kind, aimed primarily at people of faith, would be a constructive effort.

Dole: Don, I would thank you for your great effort. George and I are just sort of bit players.

One reason I got involved in this book is that it is hard to get Congress to focus on something that is happening some ten thousand miles away. There is nobody in Washington, D.C., from African countries to lobby for certain food programs. They probably cannot afford to engage people who do that for a living. So it is easy for somebody in Congress to say, "Well, nobody's bothered me about this. Nobody's talked to me about this. Why should I worry about it?" There has got to be some way. Maybe we do it through our churches. They can be very effective in lobbying—they could have a special section where they would organize and petition Congress or petition the state legislatures. If they are dealing with hunger in their own state, they will want to work on the legislature. If they are dealing with international hunger, they will want to work with Congress. But it is pretty easy to forget about domestic or world hunger. I know from experience. If nobody educates the members of Congress about it, how would they have any real concern? Maybe they will see something on television, but we've just got to keep pestering people until they get the message.

Messer: The Child Nutrition Foundation recently honored both of you for your tireless efforts for ending hunger in the world. Former presidents Bill Clinton, George Bush, and Jimmy Carter sent words of congratulations and appreciation for your determination. George,

I especially liked the way you ended your acceptance speech. It epitomizes the spirit of political bipartisanship and theological thinking that inspired this book and seeks to motivate people of faith to act in making hunger history. Would you sing it once again?

McGovern: He's got the whole wide world in his hands
    He's got all the hungry children in his hands
    He's got the Child Nutrition Foundation in his hands
    He's got Bob and Elizabeth Dole in his hands
    He's got the whole wide world in his hands.

Questions for Reflection

1. If you were to ask the authors a question about making hunger history, what would it be?

2. What concerns, if any, do you have about genetically engineered foods?

3. In relation to hunger in the world, how do you view the threats of international terrorism and global HIV/AIDS?

4. Modern philosopher Karl Popper once described plans to end poverty as reflecting either "utopian social engineering" or "piecemeal democratic reform." How would you characterize the ideas for ending hunger presented in this book?

5. What do you think the role of the church and other faith communities should be in combating hunger both domestically and internationally?

Recommended Reading

For updated information relating to hunger and global HIV/AIDS, check the International Food Policy Research Institute: www.ifpri.org.

Borlaug, Norman E. "Twentieth Century Lessons for the Twenty-first Century World." In Colin G. Scanes and John A. Miranowski, eds., *Perspectives in World Food and Agriculture 2004*. Ames: Iowa State University Press, 2004.

Monke, Jim. "Agroterrorism: Threats and Preparedness: Congressional Research Service Report for Congress." August 13, 2004. Online: www.fas.org/irp/crs/RL32521.pdf

Pinstrup-Andersen, Per. "Achieving the 2020 Vision in the Shadow of International Terrorism." In Colin G. Scanes and John A. Miranowski, eds., *Perspectives in World Food and Agriculture 2004*. Ames: Iowa State University Press, 2004.

Sachs, Jeffrey D. *The End of Poverty: Economic Possibilities for Our Time*. New York: Penguin, 2005.

What good is it, my brothers and sisters, if you say you have
faith but do not have works? Can faith save you? If a brother
or sister is naked and lacks daily food, and one of you says to
them, "Go in peace; keep warm and eat your fill," and yet you
do not supply their bodily needs, what is the good of that?
So faith by itself, if it has no works, is dead.
  —James 2:14-17

Lord, to those who hunger, give bread.
And to those who have bread, give the hunger for justice.
  —Latin American prayer

5. More Than Random Acts of Kindness

Donald E. Messer

I KNOW A PERSON WHO EVERY DAY
prepares two sandwiches for lunch at work. One he eats himself, and
the other he gives to the homeless man who sits on the street near his
high-rise business complex. I admire his commitment to feeding a
hungry person. His family's faithfulness in caring for this individual

is commendable, and I am embarrassed by my own lack of systematic personal attention to persons in need.

Without denigrating the sincerity and substance of this genuine and generous approach to sharing, it is yet evident that hunger in the United States and throughout the world requires more than random acts of kindness. However well-intended, this daily gift is a reminder of the disparity of power between the rich and the poor as well as the limits of a society based simply on charity rather than on justice. The right to eat in a world overflowing with God's abundant food ought not to be dependent on random kindness or fortuitous benevolence. No matter how good-hearted the food donor is, the recipient is reduced to five sandwiches a week and none on holidays.

Jesus commended the Good Samaritan for his action in providing care for the man who was beaten and left by robbers (Luke 10:25-37). What he did was especially meritorious, considering how priests and Levites were apparently too busy and self-absorbed. Probably they were neither evil people, nor even lacking compassion, but maybe, like me, they tended to be too caught up in their own lives to be concerned about the lives of others. Possibly they were even promoting some grand scheme to save people from abuse along the highways. But in the process they, like some of us, forgot to care for the immediate person in need.

A Good Samaritan in our era must not only give personal attention to the wounded, but be committed to finding practical personal and political ways of preventing highway muggings. When it comes to ending hunger in our time, Good Samaritans must not only share something specific and personal, but also be involved socially and politically. Only then can love and justice appropriately be expressed. As television journalist and social commentator Bill Moyers observes:

> Charity is commendable; everyone should be charitable. But justice aims to create a social order in which, if individuals choose not to be charitable, people still don't go hungry, unschooled or sick without care. Charity depends on the vicissitudes of whim

and personal wealth; justice depends on commitment instead of circumstance. Faith-based charity provides crumbs from the table; faith-based justice offers a place at the table.[1]

This chapter endorses random acts of kindness, while at the same time encouraging all of us to do far more. We need to rethink certain traditional religious practices and reappropriate biblical and theological imperatives related to social justice and combating world hunger. Charity and justice are not matters of "either/or" but of "both/and." Individuals and faith communities need to develop and implement a practical theological strategy that embraces both personal involvement and political commitment to ending hunger in our time.

Creating Political Will and Compassion Without Borders

In the last twenty to thirty years, the campaign to end hunger in the world has moved from profound pessimism to sanguine optimism, from self-defeating despair to self-fulfilling hope. When my coauthors, George McGovern and Bob Dole, were in the prime of their United States senatorial careers, they faced forecasts of dire world famine, massive overpopulation, and triage medical ethics that would require masses of people in India, Ethiopia, and Bangladesh simply to starve. Not only did some academicians and politicians join in the doomsday scenario that increasing hunger was inevitable, but a few religious ethicists lent their voices to suggest that feeding the hungry was unethical if it contributed to global overpopulation and greater world hunger. One popular Christian ethicist at the time even went as far as to say that in certain situations giving food was "immoral"[2] and there was "good and sufficient reason to 'let 'em starve.'"[3]

Yet Dole and McGovern persisted in their vision that feeding the hungry of the world was not only morally right but also technically possible. What was required then—and now—was what David Beckmann of Bread for the World calls "the political will to overcome hunger" as well as "compassion that knows no borders."[4]

Slowly emerging today is an international consensus that hunger is no longer a politically tolerable human condition. During the

2000 United Nations Millennium Summit, world leaders committed themselves to a series of ambitious and specific targets to conquer hunger. Of paramount importance is the 2015 goal of decreasing by one half the number of people suffering from hunger and lack of safe drinking water. Hunger, disease, and poverty must be addressed now, and no longer left at the end of every political priority list. In a world beset by HIV/AIDS and the threat of terrorism, the safety of every human being on the planet depends on food security for all, not just for some. Article 25 of the Universal Declaration of Human Rights beckons people of faith to advocacy and activism:

> Everyone has the right to a standard of living adequate for the health and well-being of himself and of his family, including food, clothing, housing and medical care and necessary social services, and the right to security in the events of unemployment, sickness, disability, widowhood, old age or other lack of livelihood in circumstances beyond his control.

A major step to "ending hunger now" is to achieve and exceed the World Food Summit (WFS) goal of reducing by half the number of malnourished people in the "continent of the hungry" by 2015. Progress is lagging, even though the WFS goal is deemed both "attainable and affordable" by food authorities at the United Nations.

A twin-track strategy is recommended: (1) interventions to improve food availability and incomes for the poor by enhancing their productive activities and (2) targeted programs that give very needy families immediate access to food. Empowering small-scale farmers to increase production for their families and communities will significantly reduce rural hunger. Simultaneously, the United Nations envisions creating "safety nets" and "cash transfer" programs for the most vulnerable people of the earth—such as pregnant and nursing mothers, infants and small children, school children, unemployed urban youth, plus the elderly, disabled, and sick, including those living with HIV/AIDS. The vision, as summarized in *The State of Food Insecurity in the World 2004* report issued by the United Nations, projects that:

Safety nets can also be woven with strands that contribute to development goals. Food banks and school feeding programmes can often be designed to boost incomes, improve food security and stimulate development in vulnerable rural communities by buying food locally from small-scale farmers. Similarly, programmes that provide food to people who attend education and training programmes can improve both their nutritional status and their employment prospects.[5]

In 2005 Professor Jeffrey D. Sachs of Columbia University, head of the Millennium Project, released a blueprint for cutting hunger and poverty. A *New York Times* editorial described the report as "a bold initiative that refuses to accept hunger as the inevitable fate of so many Africans, Latin Americans and Asians."[6] Industrial nations are urged to double aid to poor countries from the current giving level of one-quarter of 1 percent to one-half of 1 percent of national incomes. Rich countries are asked to support a "crash development program" immediately in at least a dozen poor but well-governed countries, like Ghana, Mozambique, Senegal, and Tanzania. Additionally, some seventeen "quick wins" were identified that would swiftly improve millions of lives. Among those cited were:

> the mass distribution of insecticide-treated bed nets to combat malaria; elimination of fees for primary education to draw the poorest children to school; expansion of school meals programs to hungry areas; distribution of de-worming medicines to schoolchildren in affected areas; and expanded treatment of people with AIDS and tuberculosis.[7]

The blueprint contends that dramatically reducing poverty in its many guises—hunger, disease, illiteracy—is "utterly affordable." Professor Sachs projects, "We're talking about rich countries committing 50 cents of every \$100 of income to help the poorest people in the world get a foothold on the ladder of development."[8]

In 2002 President George W. Bush and many world leaders supported a declaration seeking to "make a concrete effort" toward a target of providing seven-tenths of 1 percent of their national incomes for development aid. A few smaller countries like Sweden, Norway, and Denmark have met that goal, while others like France, Britain, and Spain have set a timetable to reach that mark. Currently the United States allocates less than two-tenths of 1 percent for aid and has no timetable for achieving the seven-tenths of 1 percent goal.[9]

This goal is threatened by an ever-tightening U.S. federal budget faced with massive deficits. At the end of 2004, organizations like Save the Children, Catholic Relief Services, and other charities reported that the federal government had suspended or eliminated programs designed to help the poor feed themselves through improvements in farming, education, and health. Lisa Kuennen of Catholic Relief Services said between 5 and 7 million people were affected by these cuts, when the organization was forced to downscale programs in Indonesia, Malawi, Madagascar, and other countries.[10]

Around the world nothing endangers the promise of ending hunger in the immediate future more than violence and war. Besides using up vast resources of money for military expenditures, war often also spreads hunger, leaving homeless refugees who are desperate for help and hope.

For example, because of civil war in the Democratic Republic of the Congo, it was estimated in 2001 that about one-third of the total population experienced hunger, with large numbers of people in the capital city of Kinshasa able to eat only once every two or three days. The wars in Afghanistan and Iraq have prompted the expenditures of billions of dollars—some calculations suggest over one billion dollars per week. Money spent on war and civil conflicts obviously could be used for other purposes. In the prophetic words spoken decades ago by President Dwight D. Eisenhower, a five-star general:

> Every gun that is made, every warship launched, every rocket fired signifies, in the final sense, a theft from those who hunger and are not fed, those who are cold and are not clothed.
>
> This world in arms is not spending money alone. It is spending the sweat of its laborers, the genius of its scientists, the hopes of its

children. . . . This is not a way of life at all, in any true sense. Under the cloud of threatening war, it is humanity hanging from a cross of iron.[11]

Besides budget cuts and war, the threat of environmental unsustainability and degradation endanger the prospect of making hunger history. Examining agricultural practices from an environmental point of view is a critical question facing Christians and other people of faith. How food is grown, processed, and distributed has an environmental impact. In Latin America invaluable rain forests have been destroyed in an often-futile attempt to increase land for cultivation or for raising cattle. Our quest for cheap coffee has led to destruction not only of ecologically rich rain forests but also of the songbirds that used to migrate between North and South America.

L. Shannon Jung notes that issues like soil erosion, salinization, groundwater contamination, climate change, pesticides, synthetic fertilizers, and petroleum-based cultivation contribute to "threatening the world's ability to feed its people. This linkage between hunger, poverty, and pollution underscores the need for sustainable agricultural practices."[12] Further he bluntly claims, "The way our food is produced, harvested, processed, and sold to us entails unsustainable cost to the earth community. This feeds into domestic (and worldwide) hunger and also into the diseased and malnourishing ways we eat."[13]

Reassessing our own lifestyles must be a constant project. Possibly all of us need to adopt some new dietary habits, like not eating chickens unjustly raised and processed or drinking only shade-grown coffee.[14] Arthur Simon suggests a variety of practical suggestions: "Perhaps you can consume less, waste less, eat, drink, drive, or air condition less. Cut down or out the use of fertilizer on your lawn. . . . Grow a vegetable garden and share the produce with those in need; or set aside for world relief the value of what you eat."[15]

Above all, Christians and other people of faith must confess our complicity in the sin of unsustainability and be committed to addressing environmental justice issues both personally and publicly.

Focusing on Women and Children

Women and children especially should be the special focus of Christians and other persons of faith. They bear the brunt of the brutality of malnutrition in today's world. Feeding the hungry can never discriminate due to gender or any other status, but particular attention must be devoted to the plight and predicament of women and children, as they are especially vulnerable and often exploited in cultures beset by poverty.

Catherine Bertini of the United Nations received the 2003 World Food Prize of $250,000; she donated it to a trust designed to promote the education and literacy of girls and women. In doing so, she emphasized the key importance of educating women and girls around the world, "since no other policy . . . can have such a maximum impact on poverty and hunger throughout the world."

Further, she noted that in the Two-Thirds world of agriculture, women are the principal farmers. For example, in sub-Saharan Africa women constitute 90 percent of the people working in processing food, getting water, and providing fuel. Women everywhere tell the World Food Program that they want food directly sent to their family, not just cash. Women are in charge of food; men typically control the money. Illustrating her point, Bertini told of a Latin American home to whom a nongovernmental organization had given a cow. The woman took care of the cow, milked it in the morning, took it to the fields where she worked while still tending the children, brought it back for milking again at night. She delivered the milk to the co-op. Additionally, she prepared all the meals for the family. Every day she did this, until it was time to collect the monthly check for the milk. Then her husband, who owned the cow, took the money![16]

Helping women generally means assisting children too. Around the world females remain the primary caregivers for little ones. Give a woman a bowl of rice, and she will likely first share it with her child. Give her some money, and she will somehow find a way to make sure others in the family benefit too.

Every religious tradition emphasizes caring for children. Christians feel a special relationship and responsibility for reaching out to hungry children. The nineteenth-century preacher and abolitionist Henry Ward Beecher once observed, "Children are the hands by which we take hold of heaven." Donald H. Dunson describes how the God of love embraces young ones:

> If you want to draw close to the creative presence of God, simply wrap your arms around the body of a small child yearning to grow. The Redeemer's heart burns with desire in the bodies of doctors and researchers struggling for a new world set free from malaria, hunger, AIDS, measles, polio, tuberculosis, diphtheria, whooping cough, and all the preventable infectious diseases that harm and kill life at its beginning. The Holy Spirit is the comforter and companion of all those children who walk the earth alone and who just yearn to be touched with the hand of love.[17]

Many ways exist for individuals and churches to reach out to women and children. While members of the United States Senate, coauthors Dole and McGovern championed school lunch programs; sponsored a supplemental nutrition program for women, infants, and children (WIC); fought for food stamps; and sought various other ways of addressing this challenge. In the United States some 27 million children participate in federal school breakfast and lunch programs. Now the McGovern-Dole International Food for Education and Child Nutrition Program envisions reaching out, for an estimated 19 cents a day, to the nearly 300 million children internationally who are in need of food.

President George W. Bush's first Secretary of Agriculture, Ann Venneman, noted that the pilot McGovern-Dole program affected nearly 7 million children in thirty-eight countries. Accomplishments she cited included increasing girls' school enrollment in Pakistan by 32 percent. In Bolivia it enhanced health services, including water disinfection, de-worming of children, and developing school gardens. In Kenya, besides feeding 1.7 million children, the program funded the building of new classrooms and housing for women teachers. In Venneman's words, "This program demonstrates America's compassion to improve the lives of children around the world."[18]

In 2003 the program served an estimated 2.2 million beneficiaries, primarily school children, but also mothers, infants, and preschool-age children. In conjunction with the U.N. World Food Program, as well as voluntary organizations like World Vision International, Catholic Relief Services, International Orthodox Christian Charities, and the American Red Cross, it has affected twenty-one countries, including Afghanistan, Albania, Bolivia, Côte d'Ivoire, Lebanon, Moldova, Nepal, Nicaragua, Pakistan, Tanzania, and Vietnam. To date, funding has not been at the level of the $300 million initially envisioned in the legislation but has fallen to $50 million. McGovern decries the decreases, saying, "It's terrible to start these programs and then stop them. There are some bad foreign-aid programs, but this one works."[19]

Decreased commitment to government assistance programs like the McGovern-Dole program and the failure of faith-based groups to making ending hunger a priority should prompt us to reflect on the questions posed long ago by Elizabeth Barrett Browning:

Do ye hear the children weeping, O my brothers . . . ?
. . . the young, young children, O my brothers,
They are weeping bitterly!
They are weeping in the playtime of the others.[20]

Living with Life's Contradictions

In addressing the global issue of hunger, we are forced to examine the contradictions many of us personally experience in life. Most of us recognize that we enjoy the "good life" of abundance, and we sense hypocrisy when we talk about hunger and yet continue to participate in a society rich in food and resources.

We are ensnared in political and economic structures seemingly beyond our control. Yet colonialism and imperialism, past and present, have directly or indirectly contributed materially to our lifestyles. While we can protest and work to change certain dimensions of globalization and other political and economic systems, we recognize that most Christians living in the more developed world benefit from these structures. These unseen processes affect not only our food supply, but also our income, investments, pensions, and so forth. It is impossible to live a pure life totally immune from the social dimensions of sin.

Some among us boldly demonstrate a simpler lifestyle, cutting back drastically on their way of life, living admirably with less wealth. But others of us find for various reasons this is not our way of life. We cannot completely justify our choices or explain our decisions, but we have to come to terms with living these contradictions. We can learn from Thomas Merton, the celebrated Roman Catholic Trappist monk, who admitted,

> I have had to accept the fact that my life is almost totally paradoxical. I have also had to learn gradually to get along without apologizing for the fact, even to myself. . . . I have become convinced that the very contradictions in my life are in some ways signs of God's mercy to me; if only because someone so complicated and so prone to confusion and self-defeat could hardly survive for long without special mercy.[21]

Central to Christian life is how we wrestle with the contradictions of life in light of Christian imperatives of love, justice, equality, and freedom. We must acknowledge that Christians in the so-called First World are enmeshed in structures that keep others poor. But we dare not baptize as Christian any particular economic ideology or single strategy for overcoming world hunger, for we recognize the imperfection of all things human.

But do we simply give in to our assigned and self-chosen bondage to social systems? Or do we struggle and seek to find ways to express ourselves in advocating with the poor, fighting unjust structures, providing service to the hungry, and transforming our own ways of living?

Few among us will ever be U.S. senators with special leverage to influence powerful governmental resources. Despite our situations in life, we can make some difference, if we use whatever means and power we have to end hunger in our time. Let us approach this challenge not as a duty or as a burden, but as "a celebration of grace," in the words of David Beckmann and Arthur Simon.[22] Even in so doing, we recognize personal and societal limitations and the dangers of the sins of both commission and omission. Yet in the spirit of the reformer Martin Luther, we must "sin bravely" and pray with Thomas Merton for God's "special mercy."[23]

Doing Something Personally Significant

In exploring the subject of global hunger, the time has come to listen to our hearts and hear what God is calling us to do in mission and ministry. Our heads are full of hunger statistics and stories, programs and politics, ideas and ideologies. Lest we be beset by paralysis of analysis, each of us must look inward in reflection, prayer, and meditation and see where the cry of the hungry has become the voice of God for us.

There is no one approach or strategy to which every Christian or person of faith must subscribe. Once we have committed ourselves to ending global hunger as an article of faith and as essential expression of our love of God and neighbor, the possibilities for making a difference know only the limitations of our will and imagination. We are called to go beyond random acts of kindness, as good as they may be. What follows is descriptive, not prescriptive, of what people of faith might do.

First, make a commitment to become personally involved. Doing something specific demonstrates that the matter of ending hunger is not just a "head thing" or theory, but a matter of the heart and soul. May the Holy Spirit lead each of us to find ways of constructive engagement with social justice issues of hunger in the United States and around the world. We will discover that we really do care and can be co-creators with God in ending hunger in our time. Others may see that the marks of people of faith are justice and compassion. Faith is not dead but comes alive in works of mercy.

People who volunteer in programs of direct service to the hungry always testify that the value of the work they do does not measure up to the benefits they derive spiritually and emotionally. People report that their lives have been transformed and their hearts gladdened, whether it has been helping in a food kitchen or pantry, delivering meals-on-wheels to the elderly or sick, writing letters to legislators, gleaning fields for leftover produce and grains, or raising funds through special walks and events. As Bishop K. H. Ting, the long-time church leader in China, aptly notes, "For millions today, 'Give us this day our daily bread,' is not a routine prayer but a desperate cry. We strive to be worthy instruments of the coming reign of God on earth, where this cry will be heard no more."[24]

Second, link our personal involvement with our spiritual faith. Being a Christian in the twenty-first century means not just testifying to the divine trinity, or articulating a particular Christology, or declaring oneself "born again" or "liberal" or whatever. Rather, as the highest priority of faith and ethics, it includes thinking, praying, and acting to end human hunger and misery.

Part of that process involves rethinking and reincorporating various traditional theological practices that remind us of our daily dependency on food and our spiritual and moral duty to share with our sister and brother in distress. Among many people of faith, these traditional practices have decreased or fallen out of favor for various reasons. Personally, I cannot boast that I have faithfully followed them all, but I think the time is past due for all of us to reexamine our ways and to reinstitute spiritual habits that are appropriate to our own growth in God's spirit.

A simple but primary way of linking personal involvement with our spiritual faith is by *regularly "saying grace" or offering a prayer at meals.* The simple spiritual gesture of giving thanks for food is increasingly neglected in many homes and rarely evidenced when eating in public places. Why any one of us should be embarrassed or hesitant to quietly say thanks in such situations is not clear, since we show no reluctance to speak openly about almost all other matters, and quiet prayer need not disturb or offend anyone else.

Of course, the danger always lurks that something becomes so routine that it becomes meaningless. Sometimes, for example, prayers at public events feel that way. But in our contemporary culture it is important to cleave to certain traditional religious practices. Otherwise they may be lost and not be replaced by any witness whatsoever of our food dependency upon God and our gratitude for the often unseen and unknown labors of forgotten sisters and brothers.

Finding ways of reinvigorating our own personal prayers of thanks and making public prayers appropriate in ecumenical and interfaith settings is a continuing challenge. In my own family, saying or singing mealtime graces like the Johnny Appleseed song ("The Lord's been good to me . . .") has become a small but significant integrating moment of faith and life. In recent years, as our family has changed and expanded to become interfaith, traditional Jewish practices such as Shabbat on Friday evenings have enriched our spiritual journey.

Less practiced in my own personal life has been the *religious tradition of fasting.* Refraining from taking food for specified periods of times, however, has been an integral dimension of spiritual life among many religious groups around the world. Clearly, fasting plays a time-honored spiritual role in Islam, Judaism, Buddhism, and Hinduism as well as Christianity.

Fasting forces us to recognize the essential need for food, which is crucial to life. By deliberately restraining from eating, we get an approximate but limited idea of what it means to be food insecure in a world of plenty. To see food everywhere but know none is available for us may help us begin to realize how the world must be seen and felt by a hungry child or a starving adult. Pastor Mark Buchanan suggests that

> if you never fast, then the whole concept of being wholly nourished and sustained by God's word will only be a nice, sweet and totally irrelevant thought. You may pay the idea lip service, but you'll be too busy licking sauce off your lips to do any more. And worse: if you never fast, you may not stand when the day of testing and temptation comes.[25]

Personally, I am good at making excuses for not fasting. In my boyhood, for example, when Catholics fasted during Lent, we Protestants sought to distinguish ourselves by joking we were giving up watermelon (which in those days could not be purchased in cold, snowy South

Dakota!) or by claiming we were adopting a "do-something-good-rather-than-give-something-up" approach. Upon reflection, however, I do not remember anything especially good that we actually did.

The pre–Vatican II Catholic practices of eating no meat on Fridays and giving up something desired during Lent may have lost some of their spiritual meaning by being required rather than recommended religious practices. In retrospect, however, they did serve to remind people of what it means to be hungry. Whether you were the pope or a peasant, at least momentarily you shared a common human experience of being deprived desired food.

Thomas Aquinas argued that virtue is really the automatic habit of doing good. By ritualizing certain behavior like fasting, we begin forming good habits amid the hustle and bustle of contemporary life. Thanks to church rituals we cherish Jesus' birth, remember his crucifixion, and celebrate his resurrection. Thanks to public rituals people take time to honor their mothers and fathers, commemorate the dead, and observe special political holidays. As Robert Hutchinson notes,

> ritual eliminates the need to depend upon spontaneous good intentions and firm resolves, and encourages good actions independent of feelings and moods. It is important, therefore, that fasting is ritualized so that it is done regularly, regardless of whether the motive is social justice or simply to lose weight.[26]

Fasting for fasting's sake, of course, may become simply an ascetic or self-centered practice unless it leads to greater empathy and compassion for those who do not have a voluntary choice about eating or not eating. A second-century church document offers a very practical approach of linking personal involvement with spiritual faith:

> On the day of your fast . . . compute the total expense of the food you would have eaten on the day on which you intended to keep a fast and give it to a widow, an orphan, or someone in need. . . . If you perform your fast, then, in the way I have just commanded, your sacrifice will be acceptable in the sight of God. . . . A service

so performed is beautiful, joyous, and acceptable in the sight of the Lord. (*Shepherd of Hermas* 5.3, 7-8)[27]

Individuals and groups can adapt this advice of the ancient Shepherd of Hermas to contemporary ways. Programs like Skip-a-Meal advocate praying for the hungry, deliberately denying oneself a meal once a week, and giving the amount saved to buy food for those in need.

A third step is advocacy and support for faith-based organizations that make a difference. Fortunately, a myriad of effective organizations are making a major difference in the campaign to end hunger both in the United States and around the world. Since the late 1970s, food pantries, soup kitchens, and food banks have multiplied in the United States to meet the overwhelming and tragic needs of the impoverished. More than 150,000 private feeding agencies have been developed in the United States to feed hungry Americans.

People of faith are raising their voices and casting their votes for political leaders who champion ending hunger. Bread for the World, for example, regularly sponsors a nationwide interdenominational Offering of Letters that focuses on the current necessary need for political action to combat hunger. By placing letters in the offering plate during church services, people are reminded that letters to Congress are an appropriate offering to God and active dimension of Christian stewardship.

Faith-based organizations and individuals are challenged to be in the forefront of advocacy and action. Every national and international religious group and denomination has some organization dedicated to eradicating hunger. It is quite impossible to list them all, but a few deserve special mention in order to illustrate what is being done. Updated information on the activities of these and other groups (listed alphabetically) are now easily accessible via the Internet.

Alliance to End Hunger (www.alliancetoendhunger.org) is a broad umbrella organization, bringing together the activities of a variety of specific nongovernmental organizations, both religious and secular, in a coordinated effort to influence public policy. Senator Bob Dole is an honorary cochair. There are now national alliances against hunger in over seventy-five countries, and a new network, the International Alliance Against Hunger has been launched under the leadership of the U.N. Food and Agriculture Organization, with support from the World Food Program and the International Fund for Agricultural Development.

America's Second Harvest (www.secondharvest.org) is a network of over 1 million volunteers who feed over 23 million Americans every year. It provides an intricate connection of more than two hundred food banks and food rescue organizations serving all fifty states, Puerto Rico, and the District of Columbia.

Bread for the World (www.bread.org) has emerged as a primary interdenominational organization for mobilizing churches across the country in the political struggle to end hunger now. Focusing particularly on public policy issues, it has become a potent political force in lobbying the U.S. Congress and the White House in addressing issues both domestically and internationally.

CARE, or *Cooperative for Assistance and Relief Everywhere* (www.careusa.org), began as a relief organization after World War II that looked beyond symptoms to underlying causes. CARE seeks to find lasting solutions to poverty and hunger.

Catholic Relief Services (www.catholicrelief.org) assists the poor and disadvantaged, alleviating human suffering, promoting development of all people, and fostering charity and justice around the world. First, direct assistance is provided, but then the poor are encouraged to help with their own development.

Church World Service (www.churchworldservice.org) organizes Christians to work together with partners to eradicate hunger and poverty and to promote peace and justice around the world. Ecumenical in spirit and strategy, it links issues such as global AIDS, hunger, development, and human rights around the world.

Episcopal Relief and Development (www.er-d.org) represents the Episcopal Church's engagement in the struggle to end hunger. Emphasis is placed on both short- and long-term approaches, including food relief, development assistance, and public policy advocacy.

Foods Resource Bank (www.foodsresourcebank.org) focuses primarily on helping people feed themselves and their families. An ecumenical Christian organization, it provides food security in the developing world through sustainable small-scale agricultural production.

Lutheran World Relief (www.lwr.org) seeks lasting solutions to poverty and injustice, compelling U.S. Lutherans to put faith into action. It addresses issues not only of hunger relief and emergencies but also of fair trade and development.

MAZON (www.mazon.org) has become a very powerful public policy advocacy voice for the American Jewish community. With educational programs and grant programs it mobilizes Jewish people but seeks to prevent and alleviate hunger among people of all faiths and backgrounds.

Oxfam America (www.oxfamamerica.org) seeks to enable poor people to exercise their right to manage their own lives. Oxfam takes a multifaceted approach to issues like hunger and global HIV/AIDS.

The Presbyterian Hunger Program (www.pcusa.org/hunger) engages Presbyterians in the fight against hunger in the United States and worldwide and includes education, food relief, development assistance, and public policy advocacy.

The Society of St. Andrew (www.endhunger.org) represents an ecumenical Christian ministry that feeds the hungry in the United States by saving fresh produce that would otherwise go to waste and giving it to the needy. They operate three main programs: the Potato Project, the Gleaning Network, and Harvest of Hope.

Stop Hunger Now (www.stophungernow.org) works as a charitable international relief organization that coordinates the distribution of food and other life-saving aid to crisis areas across the globe. Since its inception, Stop Hunger Now has provided more than $25 million worth of aid to people in more than forty-eight countries worldwide.

United Methodist Committee on Relief (http://gbgm-umc.org/umcor), UMCOR, is an international humanitarian aid organization operated for more than fifty years by the United Methodist Church. It has worked in more than one hundred countries, bringing hope, providing relief from hunger and disasters, and teaching peace.

World Vision International (www.wvi.org) is a well-known Christian relief and development organization working for the welfare of all people, especially children. Globally, it provides emergency relief, education, health care, and economic development and promotes justice. Considerable attention is devoted to addressing HIV and AIDS. Additional links to hunger organizations can be found at www.endinghungernow.org.

A fourth step challenges us to get others involved in the fight for a hunger-free world. Faith-based groups cannot solve the hunger crisis alone, but the world cannot resolve it unless every church, synagogue, mosque, and temple are somehow engaged in raising awareness, encouraging charity, championing social justice, offering direct services, and advocating greater governmental commitment.

Some churches set aside at least one Sunday a month to accept food offerings and emphasize the needs of the hungry. Young people can become involved in programs like World Vision's "Thirty-Hour Famine" (www.30hourfamine.org) and the Souper Bowl of Caring (www.souperbowl.org), which coincides with America's popular football extravaganza. The latter prompted 9,501 organizations to raise $3,382,155 for local food charities in 2005.

One creative and fun way of engaging children and youth in the global struggle against hunger is to introduce them to an action-packed humanitarian video game created by the U.N. World Food Program. Easy to download, www.food-force.com enables players to earn points by providing emergency relief aid to a fictitious island of Sheylan. Lesson plans for teachers, up-to-date information on the real world hunger crisis, and recommendations as to what young people can do to create a hunger-free world are included.

Another specific way of encouraging broad-based involvement is to develop educational efforts and specific action programs around the annual Hunger Awareness Day during the first week of June sponsored by America's Second Harvest. The World Hunger Program of the Evangelical Lutheran Church in America is very specific in how even small gifts can make a difference. Its Web site notes that:

- 25 cents will provide a day's supply of emergency food to a malnourished child in the Sudan
- $2 will provide one Rwandan child dinner for four weeks

- $5 will supply a day's supply of emergency food for twenty-five children
- $10 will provide enough maize, beans, and peanut seeds for a subsistence farm to start over
- $25 can help a mother in Bangladesh stock a little store with items her neighbors are sure to buy. With the profit she will be able to satisfy the needs of her hungry family.
- $34 will provide basic food for one family for two months (rice, corn, oil, sugar, and salt) in Mozambique, Africa, and
- $150 will purchase one ton of nutritious beans for emergency feeding after a disaster.[28]

Marching toward a Hunger-Free World

Too often churches, as well as society, have their priorities confused. Colin Morris years ago told how a Zambian dropped dead literally a few yards from his doorstep. "The pathologist said he'd died of hunger. In his shrunken stomach were a few leaves and what appeared to be a ball of grass. And nothing else."[29] On the same day he received a report full of controversy about the possible merger of the Anglican and Methodist Churches. Clearly the church was focused on minor issues and not responding to the fact that the poor were dying outside pastors' doors. Church divisions and denominations were triumphing rather than mission and ministry directed toward resolving the real issues facing humanity.

At this moment in time, every denomination, religious group, ecumenical organization, and interfaith partnership needs to link arms with governments and nongovernmental organizations to reverse the global trends of increased hunger and malnourishment. Let us march together toward a hunger-free world. In the words of Spanish poet Federico Garcia Lorca, "the day that hunger is eradicated from the earth, there will be the greatest spiritual explosion the world has ever known. Humanity cannot imagine the joy that will burst into the world on the day of that great revolution." Ending hunger now represents not the reach of a utopian dream, but a realistic vision within humanity's grasp.

Questions for Reflection

1. In addressing issues of world hunger, how do you think you and your church should be involved in acts of both charity and justice?

2. What approaches or strategies do you personally embrace and publicly advocate for ending hunger now?

3. In what ways do you find yourself as a person of faith experiencing life's contradictions?

4. How will you link your personal faith and religious rituals with efforts to conquer hunger? What are you willing to do?

Recommended Reading

Check the Web site of Bread for the World (www.bread.org) for updates on how Christians can lobby U.S. decision-makers about issues of justice for the world's hungry people.

Dunson, Donald H. *No Room at the Table: Earth's Most Vulnerable Children.* Maryknoll, N.Y.: Orbis, 2003.
Jung, L. Shannon. *Food for Life: The Spirituality and Ethics of Eating.* Minneapolis: Fortress Press, 2004.

Notes

Introduction

1. Celia W. Dugger, "Africans' Bleak Lives Getting Worse, Report Says," *San Francisco Chronicle*, July 16, 2004, A6.

2. Donald E. Messer, *Breaking the Conspiracy of Silence: Christian Churches and the Global AIDS Crisis* (Minneapolis: Fortress Press, 2004), 144-45.

3. Robert J. Dole, "Ending Hunger: The Politics and the Rationale," speech presented at Dakota Wesleyan University, November 21, 2002, 4.

4. June Kim quoted in Linda Green, "Beating Global Hunger Requires Political Leadership, Report Says," *United Methodist News Service*, April 14, 2004.

5. Arlene Mitchell, quoted in Daniel B. Schneider, "Take Books, Add Food, Watch the World Change," *The New York Times*, November 17, 2003, 12.

6. David Beckmann quoted in Green, "Beating Global Hunger."

7. George S. McGovern, *The Third Freedom: Ending Hunger in Our Time* (New York: Simon & Schuster, 2001), 11.

8. George McGovern quoted in Lyric Wallwork Winik, "Intelligence Report: Just 19 Cents Can End Hunger," *Parade*, March 28, 2004.

9. See Craig L. Nessan, *Give Us This Day: A Lutheran Proposal for Ending World Hunger*, Lutheran Voices (Minneapolis: Augsburg Fortress, 2003).

Chapter 1: The New Urgency of an Old Challenge

1. Cited in many sources, including the Peace Media Research Center; online: http://peace-journalism.com/ReadArticle.asp?ArticleID=2767.

2. Food and Agriculture Organization, in *The State of Food Insecurity in the World 2004* (Rome: United Nations, 2004), estimated that "852 million people worldwide were undernourished in 2000–2002. This figure includes 815 million in developing countries, 28 million in the countries in transition and 9 million in the industrialized countries" (6).

3. Statistic from U.S. Senator Elizabeth Dole, "Third Annual Hunger Awareness Day," statement to U.S. Senate, June 3, 2004.

4. Statistics cited online: www.stophungernow.org.

5. Adam Smith, *The Theory of Moral Sentiments*, 1759.

6. Sabinda Castelfranco, "Pope John Paul Urges Peace, Defense of Life and Feeding the Hungry," *VOA News*, January 10, 2005; online: www.voanews.com/english/2005-01-10-voa25.cfm.

7. See "Basic Facts about World Hunger" online: www.elca.org/hunger/facts/facts.html.

8. U.S. Senator Elizabeth Dole, "Remarks on Efforts to Address Hunger in North Carolina", *U.S.*, June 5, 2003, 5.

9. Alan Berg, *The Nutrition Factor: Its Role in National Development* (Washington, D.C.: Brookings Institution, 1973), 9.

10. *The State of Food Insecurity in the World 2004*, 28. See also Catherine Bertini, "Educate Girls: The 2003 World Food Prize Laureate Lecture," 2003 World Food Prize International Symposium, October 16-17, 2003. Online: www.worldfoodprize.org/Symposium/2003/03presentations/bertini.htm.

11. Richard Harris, "In Some Areas, Clean Water a Problem Before," National Public Radio News, January 10, 2004.

Notes 109

12. Dole, "Third Annual Hunger Awareness Day." See also David Beckmann and Arthur Simon, *Grace at the Table: Ending Hunger in God's World* (New York: Paulist, 1999), 24ff.

13. Beckmann and Simon, *Grace at the Table*, 32-33.

14. Marian Wright Edelman speaking at the Presidential Candidates' Forum on Children, Children's Defense Fund, May 9, 2003; online: www.childrensdefense.org/pdf/forum_transcript.pdf.

15. Alicia Caldwell, "Hard Times Leave Students Hungry," *The Denver Post*, January 2, 2005.

16. Sam Hananel, "Hungry, Homeless Figures Increase in U.S.," Associated Press, December 14, 2004.

17. See Donald E. Messer, *Breaking the Conspiracy of Silence: Christian Churches and the Global AIDS Crisis* (Minneapolis: Fortress Press, 2004).

18. Colin Powell, speech to United Nations General Assembly, cited in Evelyn Leopold, "U.S. Will Contribute More to Global AIDS Fund," Reuters NewMedia, June 25, 2001; online: www.aegis.com/news/re/2001/RE010673.html.

19. Food and Agriculture Organization of the United Nations, *The State of Food Insecurity in the World 2003* (Rome: United Nations, 2003), 11.

20. Donald H. Dunson, *No Room at the Table: Earth's Most Vulnerable Children* (Maryknoll, N.Y.: Orbis, 2003), 50.

21. Food and Agriculture Organization of the United Nations, *The State of Food Insecurity in the World 2004* (Rome: United Nations, 2004), 29.

22. *The State of Food Insecurity in the World 2003*, 11.

23. David J. Smith, *If the World Were a Village: A Book about the World's People* (Toronto: Kids Can, 2002), 17.

24. Smith, *If the World Were a Village*, 18.

25. Walter Harrelson, "Famine in the Perspective of Biblical Judgments and Promises," in George R. Lucas Jr. and Thomas W. Ogletree, eds., *Lifeboat Ethics: The Moral Dilemmas of World Hunger* (New York: Harper & Row, 1976), 84.

26. Robert Hutchinson, *What One Christian Can Do about Hunger in America* (Chicago: Fides/Claretian, 1982), 7-8.

27. David Beckmann and Arthur Simon, *Grace at the Table: Ending Hunger in God's World* (New York: Paulist, 1999).

28. Harrelson, "Famine in the Perspective of Biblical Judgments and Promises," 92.

29. L. Shannon Jung, *Food for Life: The Spirituality and Ethics of Eating* (Minneapolis: Fortress Press, 2004), 106.

30. See C. Dean Freudenberger and Paul M. Minus Jr., *Christian Responsibility in a Hungry World* (Nashville: Abingdon, 1976), 45.

31. Cited in Richard Schwartz, "Judaism, Hunger, and Vegetarianism," n.d.; online: www.jewishveg.com/schwartz/hunger.html.

32. Cited by W. Stanley Mooneyham, *What Do You Say to a Hungry World?* (Waco, Tex.: Word, 1975), 29.

33. Dietrich Bonhoeffer, *Ethics* (New York: Macmillan, 1955), 137.

34. John Hall Snow in "Biblical Justice and World Hunger," in Dieter Hessel, ed., *Beyond Survival: Bread and Justice in Christian Perspective* (New York: Friendship, 1977), 13.

35. Cited by Joseph A. Grassi, *Broken Bread and Broken Bodies: The Lord's Supper and World Hunger* (Maryknoll, N.Y.: Orbis, 1985), 105.

36. See especially Grassi, *Broken Bread and Broken Bodies*.

37. Barbara Brown Taylor, *Teaching Sermons on Suffering* (Nashville: Abingdon Press, 1998), 40.

38. *The Journey*, by Nancy Telfer. © 1982 Gordon V. Thompson. All rights reserved. Used by permission of Alfred Publishing Co., Inc. Miami, Florida 33014.

39. Jung, *Food for Life*, 91.

40. Craig L. Nessan, *Give Us This Day; A Lutheran Proposal for Ending World Hunger*, Lutheran Voices (Minneapolis: Augsburg Fortress, 2003), 60.

41. See Jung, *Food for Life*, 59.

42. Frances Moore Lappé, "Fantasies of Famine," *Harper's* (February 1975), 52, 54, 89.

43. Nessan, *Give Us This Day*, 52-55.

44. Ibid., 59.

Chapter 2: Ending World Hunger

1. Bono cited in "Geldof, Bono Praise G-8 for Africa AID," July 8, 2005, Associated Press, Yahoo! News. www.bradenton.com/mld/bradenton/entertainment/12120152.htm

2. The following pages of this chapter are adapted from George McGovern, *The Third Freedom: Ending Hunger in Our Time* (New York: Simon and Schuster, 2001). Printed by permission. For more extensive understanding of McGovern's perspectives, readers are encouraged to explore this book.

Chapter 3: A Commitment to Ending Global Hunger

1. This chapter is an expanded version of Senator Dole's speech, "Ending Hunger: The Politics and the Rationale," presented at Dakota Wesleyan University, November 21, 2002.

2. Elizabeth Dole quoted in accepting the Mickey Leland Emerging International Hunger Leader Award, in "Dole Receives Award," February 14, 2005, *The News and Observer* (Raleigh, North Carolina).

3. David Beckmann quoted in Juliana Finucane, "Coalition Releases 'Blueprint' It Says Can End Hunger," Bread for the World press release, June 4, 2004.

4. This joint proposal was widely cited in the press in 2002. Sources of the proposal are George McGovern, "The Healing in Helping the World's Poor," *The New York Times*, January 1, 2002, and George McGovern, "Yes, We Can Feed the World's Hungry," *Parade*, December 16, 2001.

5. Congressman Jim McGovern of Massachusetts, speaking to the U.S. House of Representatives, October 16, 2001, "America Should Provide Meals and Education for the World's Needy Children."

6. Joaquim Chissano, John Agyekum Kufuor, and Peter McPherson, "The Right Way to Aid Africa," *The Wall Street Journal*, July 5, 2002, A12.

7. Chissano, Kufuor, and McPherson, "The Right Way to Aid Africa."

8. See Bob Dole, "A Reflection of America," farewell address to the United States Senate, June 11, 1996.

9. "A Message from Bob Dole and Leon Panetta," in Bread for the World's 2005 Offering of Letters.

10. American Special Supplemental Food Program for Women, Infants, and Children (WIC) provides food, nutrition counseling, and access to health services for breast-feeding and low-income pregnant women, other postpartum women, young children, and infants who are at nutritional risk. Legislation, first passed in 1972, was co-sponsored by the late Senator Hubert Humphrey, Senator George McGovern, and Senator Bob Dole.

11. See "Ending Hunger: The Politics and the Rationale," unpublished speech, Dakota Wesleyan University, November 21, 2002.

12. Bob Dole and George McGovern in "One Lunch at a Time," *Washington Post*, May 1, 2002, A23.

13. Prepared testimony by Senator Bob Dole to the Senate Agriculture, Nutrition, and Forestry Committee, July 27, 2000.

14. Senator Bob Dole cited by the Food Research and Action Center.

15. "A Message from Bob Dole and Leon Panetta."

16. Ibid.

Chapter 5: More Than Random Acts of Kindness

1. Bill Moyers, foreword to Jim Wallis, *Faith Works: How Faith Based Organizations Are Changing Lives, Neighborhoods, and America* (New York: Random House, 2000).

2. Joseph Fletcher, "Give If It Helps But Not If It Hurts," in William Aiken and Hugh La Follette, eds., *World Hunger and Moral Obligation* (Englewood Cliffs, N.J.: Prentice-Hall, 1977), 105.

3. Joseph Fletcher, "Feeding the Hungry: An Ethical Appraisal," in George R. Lucas Jr. and Thomas W. Ogletree, eds., *Lifeboat Ethics: The Moral Dilemmas of World Hunger* (New York: Harper & Row, 1976), 58. See also Paul and William Paddock, *Famine 1975* (Boston: Little, Brown, 1968); Paul Ehrlich, *The Population Bomb* (New York: Ballantine, 1971); and Garrett Hardin, "Lifeboat Ethics: The Case against Helping the Poor," *Psychology Today,* September, 1974.

4. David Beckmann, "Ending Hunger in America," 2003 World Food Prize International Symposium, October 16–17, 2003. Online: www.worldfoodprize.org/Symposium/2003/03presentations/beckmann.htm

5. Food and Agriculture Organization, *The State of Food Insecurity in the World 2004* (Rome: United Nations, 2004), 33.

6. Editorial, "A Proposal to End Poverty," *The New York Times,* January 22, 2005.

7. Celia W. Dugger, "U.N. Panel Urges Doubling of Aid to Cut Poverty," *The New York Times,* January 18, 2005.

8. Ibid.

9. Ibid.

10. Elizabeth Becker, "U.S. Cuts Global Food Aid As Budget Shrinks," *Denver Post,* December 22, 2004, 2A.

11. Dwight D. Eisenhower, quoted in George McGovern, *The Third Freedom: Ending Hunger in Our Time* (New York: Simon & Schuster, 2001), 112.

12. L. Shannon Jung, *Food for Life: The Spirituality and Ethics of Eating* (Minneapolis: Fortress Press, 2004), 88.

13. Ibid.

14. See Kent D. Messer, Matthew J. Kotchen, and Michael R. Moore, "Can Shade-Grown Coffee Help Tropical Biodiversity? A Market Perspective," *Endangered Species Update* 17/3 (November/December 2000): 50-72.

15. Arthur Simon, *Bread for the World* (New York: Paulist Press, and Grand Rapids, Mich.: Wm. B. Eerdmans Publishing Co., 1975), 170.

16. See Catherine Bertini, "Educate Girls: The 2003 World Food Prize Laureate Lecture," 2003 World Food Prize International Symposium, October 16-17, 2003. Online: www.world-foodprize.org/Symposium/2003/03presentations/bertini.htm.

17. Donald H. Dunson, *No Room at the Table: Earth's Most Vulnerable Children* (Maryknoll, N. Y.: Orbis Books, 2003), 10.

18. See "U.S. Launches Global Feeding Program for School Children," U.S. Department of State, International Information Programs, March 11, 2003: online: http://usinfo.state.gov/usa/pr031103.htm. Also Daniel B. Schneider, "Take Books, Add Food, Watch the World Change, *The New York Times,* November 17, 2003, 12.

19. George McGovern, quoted in Lyric Wallwork Winik, "Intelligence Report: Just 19 Cents Can End Hunger," *Parade,* March 28, 2004.

20. Elizabeth Barrett Browning, "The Cry of the Children," in *The Complete Poetical Works of Elizabeth Barrett Browning* (New York: Houghton Mifflin, 1900), 156-58.

21. Thomas P. McDonnell, ed., *A Thomas Merton Reader* (Garden City, N.Y.: DoubleDay/ Image Books, 1974), 16.

22. David Beckmann and Arthur Simon, *Grace at the Table: Ending Hunger in God's World* (New York: Paulist, 1999), 6.

23. This section draws upon the author's understanding of an "enslaved liberator" image of ministry. See Donald E. Messer, *Contemporary Images of Christian Ministry* (Nashville: Abingdon, 1989), 135-52.

24. K. H. Ting, "The Cry for Bread," republished in Raymond L. Whitehead, ed., *No Longer Strangers: Selected Writings of K. H. Ting* (Maryknoll, N.Y.: Orbis, 1989), 72.

25. See Jung, *Food for Life*, 110n.17.

26. Robert Hutchinson, *What One Christian Can Do about Hunger in America* (Chicago: Fides/Claretian, 1982), 104.

27. Quoted in Joseph A. Grassi, *Broken Bread and Broken Bodies: The Lord's Supper and World Hunger* (Maryknoll, N.Y.: Orbis, 1985), 93.

28. Online: www.elca.org/hunger/facts/facts.html.

29. Colin Morris, *Include Me Out! Confessions of an Ecclesiastical Coward* (London: Epworth, 1968), 39-41.

Index

Scriptural Index